# An Actor's Place

©2000 Pelham McMahon

Published by The Bluecoat Press, Liverpool
Book design by March Design, Liverpool
Printed by GZ Printek, Spain

**Front cover** On stage rehearsal of the 1963 production of 'The Entertainer' by John Osborne, directed by David Scase. Frederick Stokes as Archie Rice on stage with David Collins, Ronnie Settle the Musical Director, Joan Ovens and Tony Colgate in the orchestra pit.

ISBN 1 872568 61 0

Thanks to: Pam Brooks, Valerie Gardiner and Sarah Walker. • The staff, past and present, especially those who saved material for the archives. Particular mention is given here to Christopher and Jackie Bullock, Henry and Sue Cotton, Bill and Dorothy Selby, Carol Walker and many others. But an especial mention must be made of Elizabeth Ann Meacham and Melanie Dodd, who had the task of ensuring the safety of information at the time of the closure. • Stanley Williams, the only surviving call boy from the 1930s. • John Arnatt, Dorothea Alexander, Karen Archer, Beryl Bainbridge, Jean Boht, Miranda Bell, Alec Bregonzi, David Beckett, Alan Bennion, Stephen Boswell, Doyne Byrd, Colin Baker, Stephen Boxer, Caroline Blakiston, Richard Briers, June Broughton, Judy Campbell, Rosalie Crutchley, Gilly Coman, Bernard Cribbins, John Challis, Trevor Danby, Ann Davies, Helen Fraser, Shelagh Fraser, Karin Fernald, Gary Files, John Franklyn-Robbins, Brenda Fricker, Damian Gaskin, Martin Scott Gilmore, Doran Godwin, David Goodland, Harold Goodwin, Anthony Higginson, Anthea Holloway, Ronald Herdman, Nadine Hanwell, Sue Jenkins, Milton Johns, Bert Kwouk, Sheila Keith, Byrony McRoberts, Steven Mathers, Alan Partington, Roger Phillips, Pamela Pitchford, Linda Polan, Michael Poole, Paul Ryan, Ronald Settle, Richard Simpson, David Suchet, Graham Stark, Hugh Tudor, Elizabeth Tyrrell, Ted Valentine, Angela Vale, Paul Williamson, Clare Welch, Benjamin Whitrow, June Watson, Kathleen Worth, Marcia Warren, Arthur Whybrow, Paula Wilcox, Richard Williams, Susan Wilson, Gilbert Wynne, Arnold Yarrow, Marjorie Yates. • Naomi Evetts and the staff of the Public Records Office, Central Library. • Michael Seagroatt, Honorary Librarian of the Athenaeum Club. • Mrs Margaret Voake, for donating her late husband's notes on the Playhouse History. • The family of Sidney Jeffery for donating his notes and for coming to speak with us. • James Rushworth, Christopher Bullock, Stanley Williams, all of whom went far beyond just responding to a request for information. They brought understanding and a sense of the past which proved invaluable. • Cathy Alger, Liz Horrigan and Michael Williams [LX] for assistance with material. • The Architects of the new building, Mr Wilson and Mr Hall. • Max Tyler, Historian of the British Old Time Music Hall Society, for useful clues to researching the history of the Old Star Theatre. • The reporters and staff at The Liverpool Daily Post and Echo, especially, Joe Riley, Phil Key, Stephen Shakeshaft and Colin Hunt of the Photo Library. • Angela Heslop, Linda McDermot of BBC Radio Merseyside. • The Stage Newspaper, especially Margery Bates Murphy. • Phil Cutts, the theatre photographer for nearly fifteen years. • Anne Gilmore, photographer and Chair of the Liverpool Photographic Society. • The National Association of Women's Clubs, who helped with anecdotes and photographs, especially St Andrew's at Clubmoor. • The Townswomen's Guild, for programmes, anecdotes, and photographs, especially the Bebington branch. • The Probus Members of Liverpool, especially the Huyton Branch. • Mr & Mrs P Breen, of Lyver & Boydell Galleries. • Miss Anne Callan for memories of the Belmont. • The Friends of the Liverpool Playhouse Society. • Miss Marjorie Tickle, Pat Burgess and Beryl Spellman and other members of the Thursday Morning History Group who collected memories from elderly neighbours and friends. • Mrs Mary Coffee (nee Aitchison) for memories of the 1930s. • Beryl Driscoll of the Wednesday Club for gathering material on the 1930s. • Joseph Staples of the Walker Art Gallery for photograph and advice. • The members of the 050 Club for help given. • The residents of Gorselands Court for memories shared. • The University of the Third Age at 126 Mount Pleasant, for programmes and memories shared. • The countless individuals who responded to our appeal for information and old programmes. • Rebe Rathbone and Viv Hughes for practical help and support. • The Blue Badge Guides and the Merseyside Tourism Office for information and advice.

# An Actor's Place

The Liverpool Repertory Company at Liverpool Playhouse, 1911 – 1998

Pelham McMahon and Pam Brooks

# CONTENTS

# FOREWORD
## By Pelham McMahon

What began as a private collection of stories and memorabilia about the Liverpool Playhouse, I used as anecdotes to enliven talks, which I gave to visitors touring the theatre. As a teacher and writer, I became known for the storytelling side of the tours, revelling in the obvious enjoyment of the various groups of adults and children to whom I was speaking. It was Caroline Parry who suggested I write a guidebook. Later, Richard Williams endorsed the suggestion that a full history book might be just as welcome. With his authority behind me, I extended my research and quickly realised the goldmine of information available to me in the archives. Sadly, try as I could, the work came too late to help save the Company. Thus it is, that this book is now a retrospective tribute to the 87 years of The Liverpool Repertory Company. On January 3rd 1998, the Company closed and The Liverpool Playhouse itself became like a beloved family home in the uneasy stages of probate - still casting the shadows and smells of loved ones departed and yet poised for revitalisation.

There had been periods when an inconsistency in the maintenance of the Theatre's records was evident, but in 1991 and 1998 all surviving records were handed over to the Liverpool Public Records Office. In researching these extensive archives, the help of Pam Brooks became a valued support to my own work and it is quite impossible to explain her faithful commitment to this project. A true lover of the Playhouse and all things theatrical, she responded with great eagerness to my appeal for research assistance. I know that there were days when she must have wondered what she had embarked upon; but perseverance is a virtue she possesses in abundance. Her "Database" was most diligently researched and greatly extended the listings, begun by Jackie Bullock, of every named actor and backstage worker. Any name missing will be the responsibility of previous archivists, for Pam has given as close a verification of the numerical facts as is possible, at this time. Pam also helped me with the editing of the text, before going on to produce a most comprehensive index. But to theatre students of the future, she will be remembered for the database she has produced. I would like to thank her for uncovering the name of the original architect of the 1866 building. For 100 years every volume written had stated the architect was unknown, but Pam's diligence paid off and another detail was added to the archive, enabling us to confirm and strengthen the research of other Liverpool theatre writers, most notably Harold Ackroyd.

There is a pattern to the book that I hope will allow the reader to dip in and out as the mood takes them. Facts and humour mixed together, whether for reference, or a few moments of reflection, as fond memories are reawakened. It touches upon many of the diverse characteristics of the life of the Company. With to date, 4,624, recorded names of actors who have appeared in nearly 2,000 productions on the main house or the studio stages, it is obvious that somewhere along the line I have had to be selective in my story telling. That is the point: I wanted to tell a story. I did not want to write just a textbook. Therefore, if it seems somewhat of an admixture of facts, or if I have missed out your favourite person, I make the barest apology. Similarly, within the text, the subsequent career development of any Company member is seldom mentioned. My interest is with the very ordinariness of true Repertory, with the ethos and management of Repertory production and its suitability for the community that supports it.

Nothing has been easy in preparing this volume. For a start, I had a choice of 44 actors named Jones, then there were 31 Smiths, 31 Williams, 23 Wilsons, 19 Roberts, and 19 Davies, and so the roll call goes on and on. It became necessary to select only a handful of known actors to feature for each decade, and to be ruthless with any attempt to effect pet changes to the contents. In the end it was those who responded with realistic anecdotes that I found to be the more useful. Blind adoration does not tell a good yarn but, with the index listing over nine hundred names, every decade has its representative heroes and heroines, with just a few naughty boy stories thrown in for good measure.

Collating the personal memories that came to light, from the response to radio or press appeals, was am amazing experience. I was confronted with the evidence of such a widespread affection for the actors and the building itself, that I just knew I was right to attempt this story. To those who helped, I do have to apologise, for I could not record so many names in the list of acknowledgements. However, those of the late Colin Voake and Sidney Jeffery appear several times in the text and I am indebted to their families for entrusting me with documentation from their estates. For Colin Voake, who died before he could begin the text of his own intended book on the theatre, we particularly hope our work brings joy to his family.

I am indebted to Naomi Evetts of the Public Records Office. To her, both Pam Brooks and I extend our thanks. Together with her colleagues, she became an essential part of our success in co-ordinating our two-pronged approach to the research. Her diligence in organising the archive must be complimented.

The research of such legal records of the Repertory Company as were available to me, and the financial records at Companies House, Cardiff and London, and any subsequent assessment of the Company's success or failure, is entirely my personal input into this story of triumph and eventual tragedy.

I have no doubt that some will find fault, that a few may feel vindicated, and that others may be reassured that the life and work of the Liverpool Repertory Company was not a total failure. Everything has its life cycle, and history is only of value if it teaches us to avoid certain pitfalls in the future. The images and lessons portrayed in this volume will hopefully establish the importance of wisdom and experience working hand in hand, assessing and strengthening each innovation brought in by successive generations. All future development at the Playhouse should strive to avoid the mistakes of the past, and there were many over the years; utilise the lessons of success, most particularly respect for the customer; and develop a style and characteristic ethos that does credit to such an historic institution.

Every effort was made to contact photographers, where they could be identified. However, any photograph used from the archive, which could not be assigned to a specific photographer, is recorded as 'From the Playhouse Archives'.

Personal thanks go to my niece, Sarah Walker for editing various drafts of the book. To Valerie Gardiner, for the encouragement given when the sheer volume of material overwhelmed both Pam and myself.

My thanks to Colin Wilkinson and his staff at The Bluecoat Press for keeping faith with me over a two-year period of preparation. With the closure of the Company at the theatre, it is his investment of time and money which has kept this project afloat. A brave man! My compliments, also to Michael March of March Design, for surviving the battle over photographs, thereby producing a visually beautiful book.

And finally to you, the reader. Hopefully you will read with love and affection my attempt to lightly cover a life that was mostly vibrant, bravely withstood political and social pressures, sometimes had ailments of its own making, and which finally faced the end with a dignity that showed its true greatness.

# STAR * MUSIC * HALL

### WILLIAMSON SQUARE, LIVERPOOL.

Proprietors and Managers — Messrs. FINEBERG & LEES.

## PROGRAMME FOR WEEK ENDING MAY 18, 1895.

1 Overture - - - **Band**

2 Mr. **FRED DARBY**
Comedian and Dancer.

3 Miss **DORA CLIFFORD**
Serio-Comic Vocalist.

4 "**The Return from Kansas**"
BY CORNISH, HARDY, SAMPSON AND BROS. SLOCUM.

5 Miss **LILLIE LANGTRY**
Burlesque Actress.

6 Mr. **WALTER KINO**
Character Comedian and Vocalist.

Grand Selection from A. Thomas' Opera,
" LE CAID ! "
By the Splendid Band of the Establishment.
Conductor - - - Mr. H. BAYMAN.

7 E MEZZETTIS
rizontal Bar Performers.

# Chapter One
## THE FOUNDATIONS 1837 — 1911

**J**em Ward 'A pugilist with a love of culture' must seem like a strange description for the character who laid down the foundations of entertainment on the site now known as 'The Liverpool Playhouse'. The 1841 census names him as James Ward, the 1844 WC Clelland water-colour of Williamson Square shows his hotel as the James Ward Hotel. The Liverpool Review of 2 August 1890, in an article entitled *Williamson Square in 1845*, speaks of him as having been called 'Jim Ward'. To quote, "Jim was once a leading man in the prize ring, but took to more peaceful ways, and not only a connoisseur in oil paintings, but himself a bit of an artist. He was a capital fellow all round and much respected. His house became a sort of local Evans', where you could hear a good song and get a chop or nice bit of supper." It would appear that Broadbent's 1908 account of 19th Century Liverpool theatres, much of which was reliant upon living memory, refers to him as Jem Ward, a name more appropriate to a fighting man. Gore's Directories of Liverpool place him as living at Number 16 Williamson Square prior to 1840. He appears to have arrived from Middlesex about 1837, and taken out the licence on the Star Inn and added his name to the fascia as seen in a Clelland water-colour of the time. This painting further verifies RJ Broadbent's [Liverpool Stages 1908] description of the building:

"Its exterior appearance was that of a dwelling house, the entrance being up some steps. Inside, the concert room consisted

of what at one time had been the front and back parlours, made into one, and at the further end was a small stage."

For a more accurate idea of their appearance, the houses of Rodney Street, many of them built about the 1770s, most nearly mirror the Star Inn at Number 16 and the premises at Number 17 Williamson Square.

At Number 17 was a bonnet factory owned and run by a Frederick Barford in 1839 – 1847 and Frederick Cox in 1847 – 1864. Described in Gore's Directories as a Straw Plait and Bonnet Warehouse, with apparent sub-lets of various floors to Oyster Rooms, general carriers, muslin sewing manufacturers and in 1865 a gun maker, it appears to have been greater in size than the Hostelry. Both the 1848 Ordnance Survey and the 1858 and 1860 Herdman water-colours of Williamson Square would confirm this.

**Williamson Square.** The square was named after Robert Williamson, the owner of the weekly *Liverpool Advertiser*, the earliest regular local newspaper, started in 1756. It was an actual square in shape, having sides of equal length of 80 feet and had main sewer pipes running down from Upper Dawson Street and from Houghton Street. These were buried about four feet below the cobbled surface of the Square. Although there would appear to have also been open gutters against the walkways at this time, it was still a more pleasant open space than others available in the city.

**The People in the Hotel.** The fact that many of the Hotel's overnight visitors were travellers, awaiting a ship's tide to the New World, adds to the endless variety of colour which characterised the life in Williamson Square at this period. Only then may we understand how Jem came to be sitting, drinking his own ale and inviting his customers to come forward to the dais to sing or dance, recite or conjure, tumble or clown, for the benefit of all. Such travellers take with them, wherever they go, an overpowering need to honour their fatherland by perpetuating its cultural heritage. Jem must have been witness to many haunting lyrics which painted the beauty of European valleys, eastern sunsets, or distressing farewells from elderly parents. That the Irish potato famine was exerting its extensive influence upon the life of the city of Liverpool cannot be disputed, and many poor and weary Irish would have stayed at The Star Inn, en route for The New World.

*Star Music Hall poster from 1895 with Lillie Langtry described as a burlesque actress.*

Similarly, as time went on, the nearness to Lime Street made the inward traveller, awaiting the morning trains, seek the conveniently placed, Star. Jem obviously enjoyed his work at the Star and extended his control to The York Hotel. [The York was situated where Stoniers once traded, on the corner of Tarleton Street.]

**The New Star Concert Hall.** It would appear that Jem had permanently removed himself to the York by 1847. After several changes of ownership and a change of name to 'The Star Hotel' in 1860 and later [1865] to The Star Concert Hall, the 1866 owners of Number 16, David Lazarus and possibly an Emmanuel Braham, purchased number 17 and built the New Star Concert Hall as an Old Time Music Hall venue. Thus the structure known today as the original theatre building, is positioned across the site of the two eighteenth century houses.

A contemporary press reference announced that the Star Hotel would close after the last show on the night of 2 July 1866, for the purpose of erecting the 'New Star Concert Hall'. This is recorded as being opened less than six months later, "… minus its exterior decoration", on 26 December 1866. The interior of the house was designed after the Oxford Music Hall Theatre, which was situated at the junction of Tottenham Court Road and Oxford Street, London. Broadbent describes the Star as follows: "For many years the Star, with … its chairman, hammer in hand, and its small tables around which the waiters dodged in and out in a marvellous manner, was a bright and alluring rendezvous for lovers of mirth and melody."

**Edward Davies – the Architect.** The architect of the New Star is now rightfully acknowledged as Edward Davies. The details of his life are briefly summed up as: "for forty years a Liverpool-based architect".

*The Toxteth grave of Edward Davies, architect of the 1866 building. [Pam Brooks]*

Research in the Public Records Office gives these details: Edward Davies was born in 1821 at an unknown address.

| His known homes | His identified offices |
| --- | --- |
| 1848 17 Phythian Street | |
| 1851 84 London Road | 22 King Street |
| 1858 Sandown Park, Wavertree | 3 Temple Court |
| 1865 10 Salisbury Terrace, Old Swan | 9 Temple Court |
| 1867 Victoria Villas, 3 Victoria Road | 4 Church Alley |
| 1890 | at this time the Company is listed as: |
| | Edward Davies and Son |
| | Architect and Surveyors |
| | at Prince Arthur Chambers |
| | 19 Sir Thomas Buildings West |

Edward Davies is credited with being involved in work on the Rotunda Theatre and with buildings on Lime Street. He died at home on 20 June1893, aged 72 and is buried in Toxteth Cemetery. His death was reported in the Liverpool Courier: "Death of an old Liverpool Architect, Mr Edward Davies who died 20 June 1893. He left a son, Mr Arthur E Davies; Mr Harold Davies, grandson; Mr Joseph Ball, son-in-law and Misses Lucy and Arabella Davies and Mrs J Ball, daughters".

**LIVERPOOL REPERTORY THEATRE**

**THE AUDITORIUM**

*Stanley Adshead's proposed interior for the auditorium. This is taken from the 1911 brochure and is his original design, only the ceiling decoration having been changed. The auditorium has been painted in various colours in its history, but the early cream walled choice did not prove popular. Since the 1930s a dark red, blue or, on one occasion, a deep purple was used as the primary colour.*

In 1896 the theatre was refurbished inside and out and in 1898 a dramatic licence was applied for, the last variety show being on 28 May 1898. Two days later, Mr Rollo Balmain's Company opened with *Hoodman Blind* with 2,000 in the audience.

The history of the theatre at this period is not relative to this volume, but one beautiful link to the present day came from Andrew Schofield, the leading Company member of the 1980s who, with great pride, recalls the fact that his grandmother once went up to sing on the stage at The Star during an open evening. His grandfather was over ninety when he told Andrew that there "… was an orchestra in the pit, but I can't remember what your grandmother sang". The original building was gas lit. There was a side entrance for gentlemen without a female to escort. There were tables and chairs within the front stage area, six red-curtained boxes either side of the proscenium arch, and a general air of red plush which Professor Sir Charles Reilly described as more in keeping with a bordello [*Scaffolding in the Sky*]. Perhaps the fact that for years the 'ladies of the night' were allowed to stand at the back of the gallery area for as little as one penny, added to the ambience of drink and lustiness which characterised early Music Hall audiences. The rear gallery prices in 1866 were 4d, similar to a day's domestic service. By the late 1940s they had risen to 9d and were increased gradually over the years until from the 1980s they were at £3.00, in line with an hour's basic wage.

The flushing toilets at the back of the gallery are believed to have been introduced or refurbished before the turn of the century, perhaps in the 1898 refurbishment, and are well remembered amongst very elderly ladies as originally having a large and attractive design of blue roses fired into the porcelain. A visit to them was considered a treat, as a great many of the gallery clientele came from homes without indoor sanitation. After considerable reticence, very elderly gentlemen admitted to the presence of a bumble-bee design, strategically placed in the gents' urinals. Whilst not as elegant as the famous Victorian toilets of the Philharmonic Eating Rooms on Hope Street, they were at the time of great importance to the theatregoers. The introduction of sanitation is believed to have been facilitated by the position of the Houghton Street and Upper Dawson Street sewers as mentioned above.

The performance space of the old building has the great advantage of giving everyone the feeling of being near the stage. It is a mere sixty feet from stage front to the back row of the upper circle. Apart from the more recent TV trained performers, many of whom have little or no experience in voice projection technique, few actors have had difficulty in being easily heard anywhere in the auditorium. As Grace Wyndham Goldie states in her 1935 volume *The Liverpool Repertory Theatre*, when speaking of the importance of the size of the theatre in relation to the work being put on, it is, "at once a cause of the theatre's success and a limitation set upon its activity" [Goldie].

**Stanley Adshead – the Interior Designer.** In 1911, when the building was purchased by the newly-formed Liverpool Repertory Theatre Company, the interior of the building was redesigned by Professor Stanley Adshead of Liverpool University. It is his work in the auditorium and stalls coffee bar which enabled the building to be listed Grade II, as of historical interest. That, and the fact that the building itself is believed to be amongst the dozen oldest complete original theatre buildings [it still has all four original walls and most of its original roof] still in use in England, will hopefully ensure its continuance.

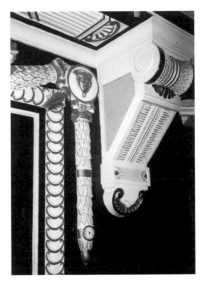

*Detail of plaster moulding above the left front stalls entrance to the auditorium. [Anne Gilmore]*

**Opposite** *Exterior building post 1959 and pre 1962. The canopies along the side and front of the theatre were much loved by those queuing for tickets. Taken down in 1966–1967, they have never been replaced as they were never part of Edward Davies' original design.*

THANK YOU VERY MUCH EVERYONE AT THE PLAYHOUSE THEATRE

*Letter from a child.*

**Opposite** [1] Rigging. [2] Some of the roof space over the stage. [3] Chandelier. [Phil Cutts] [4] Prompt Desk. [5] Box office in 1866 Foyer. [6] The old boiler. [7] A dressing room with Suzanne Riley of the National Association of Womens Clubs. [8] The Victorian Rain Machine. [9] New Paint frame from 1966. [10] One of the prop rooms. [11] The Friends' costume hire wardrobe. [Gilmore]

**Heritage tours of the building.** The heritage tours and open days of the 1980s and 1990s clearly highlighted the public's delight with the many anecdotes surrounding the building itself. Popular features were:

▶ the rope rigging of the stage. The original rigging was done by ship's riggers from the docks;

▶ if a member of the stage management department was available, visitors were frequently shown how to operate the iron [fire safety curtain] or the rigging or the prompt desk 'traffic light' system;

▶ the 'grey lady' corridor, in fact part of the 1966 extension and an entirely fictitious ghost invented to keep children quiet when walking near the rehearsal studio;

▶ the chandelier's loss of its crystal sides, some of it caused by a badly-aimed air gun pellet. It was not until 1973 that fibreglass was fitted.

▶ the gas fitting in the old Foyer [the theatre had gas as secondary lighting until the 1960s].

▶ in 1866, the gallery was accessible from the Dress Circle via a hidden door behind one of the gallery box offices. These are not believed to have been used since the early 1950s, unlike the old foyer box offices, which have not been in use since 1968, following the opening of the extension. The old foyer box office on the left, with access to the theatre auditorium, was for advance booking and usually the only one open during the day. The one on the right, which was little more than a cupboard, was opened about seven for that evening's performance.

▶ it was usually not possible to show tour groups into the roof spaces, but small groups could sometimes be taken through, if the fire officer was in attendance,

▶ access to the under stage area for smaller groups was always a highlight of the tours. Bemused by the old gas boiler, the LX department, the 'gel' room, the large prop storage area and the many lanterns hanging between the old railway sleepers which support the sprung stage in the basement, visitors moved into a reality of backstage life seldom accurately portrayed in films.

They could clearly see the three trap doors to stage front, one of which is recorded as the scene of an accident involving Gertrude Lawrence. It was sometimes difficult to move the tour groups on from the Victorian rain machine, because everyone seemed to have a wish to 'make it rain'! Thunder was originally created by running a metal ball down a long zig-zagging slide in the roof space above the audience. As it rolled, the growling of the thunder was heard, as it crashed into the turns, the loud claps of thunder would deafen the audience. It was removed once taped sound effects came into fashion.

▶ Eventually visitors would find their way to the old dressing rooms (Rooms C, J, K, L) which, small and with their windows now bricked up, retain the true impression of the cramped conditions of the 1866 building, when every available cubby hole was used as a dressing room, including spaces above the two boxes in the auditorium – accessed via gantries across the roof space of the stage.

Dressing up for Open Day was part of the fun for those who helped and those just visiting backstage. The St Andrew's Club [NAWC] and many other organisations were frequent helpers. The Friends of the Liverpool Playhouse extended these activities to include a costume hire service. Sometimes difficult to man with volunteer labour, it nevertheless provided considerable help, especially to schools.

The 1866 stone cupolas each weighed over a ton and caused structural damage to the corner staircases to the gallery. In the late 1960s they were replaced with fibreglass copies. [Liverpool Daily Post and Echo]

The new developments by the architects Wilson, Hall and Donoghue extended the building to include a new box office, a new workshop, alterations to the stage and backstage areas, such as a new green room and more dressing rooms. The new paint frame was set above the workshop, as was the room which eventually became known as 'The Theatre Upstairs' or later, as 'The Studio'. Significantly, the introduction of a restaurant area inside the largest of the glass drums was to become a source of recurring headaches to the Board as different franchises came and went for the next thirty years.

The 1966 – 1968 extension had the added interest of the views across Williamson Square. To the left, from the Star Bar on the top level, could be seen the cupolas on the old theatre building, now modern fibreglass replacements for the one hundred year old originals.

This volume did not set out to limit itself to just the building, as much of the subject has been dealt with elsewhere [*The Liverpool Playhouse Tour Guidebook*, by Pelham McMahon, not currently in print, and *The Liverpool Stages* by Harold Ackroyd].

Tours often ended with a cup of coffee, sometimes in the Stalls Coffee Lounge downstairs, where one final story always interested adult visitors. During the matinee on the afternoon of 18 November 1967, a few minutes after the end of the interval, the ceiling of the coffee bar fell down. This was caused by several layers of plastering having been weakened by the vibration from the building work on St John's Lantern. Because the lights were flickering, Michael Williams, one of the electricians on duty that day, was called down to the bar. A severe cracking noise was heard and patches of the ceiling were seen to be dipping rather alarmingly. When it all fell in, neither Michael nor Doris Houlton, the usher on coffee duty, was harmed, but if it had happened minutes earlier, the area would have been packed with members of the audience, some of whom would surely have been injured. The immediate fear was that the whole theatre was about to collapse and so the General Manager decided to stop the play and ask the audience to leave, for their own safety. The actors on stage did not know the reason for the evacuation, but Anthea Holloway had the presence of mind to talk to the audience, as they were filing out, to allay any signs of panic. Only after everyone had left, was she able to hear what had happened. Michael Williams spoke of the horsehair found in the original layer of plaster and of the many wine bottle corks which had fallen out of the cavity, between the plaster and the floor of the auditorium above. Whether these corks were used as early sound insulation, or whether they had fallen through into the space below the auditorium floor-boards in the Old Time Music Hall days of 1866 to 1897, when wine was served to the audience as they sat around small tables, no one will ever know for certain. A mystery of history, yet a story which still delights those who tour the building. The damage was made good within forty-eight hours and the theatre reopened on the Monday for business as usual.

Less visible in terms of damage is the effect of the high water table beneath the theatre. The loss of manufacturing industry in the city has meant a rise in the natural water table below the theatre. This is mostly controlled by pumping and air conditioning. The damage from the burst water tank above the auditorium, on 18 May 1994, did however severely affect two productions, *Feed* starring Roy Barraclough and *Reet Petite*. The later was transferred to the Everyman Theatre for its entire run.

The stalls coffee bar was originally, in 1866, the beer cellar. The draymen delivered the ale down a chute from Houghton Street. The display cabinet by the stairs to the auditorium now covers this chute. The picture shows the Adshead decoration. which is mostly still intact except for the ceiling.

**The future of the building.** The building is currently [2000] facing repair and alterations, the plans for which may be viewed with some suspicion, because in the light of the research for this book, historical precedents have shown that access to backstage must not limit the work of either in-house or touring productions. With no rear 'vista' stage space to support scene changes, the provision of stage-right access into the current workshop area is imperative. The greater the loss of floor space in the workshop area, the greater the risk of faulty access and the possibility of a final coup de grâce to the theatre itself.

**The end of the Liverpool Repertory Company.** How much of the building will survive to sustain the work of future theatre practitioners remains to be seen, but one thing is certain, the Company which gave spirit to the last 86 years, so unique in the history of Repertory, has gone for good. It might seem selfish to complain about the loss of the controlling Company at the Playhouse but, the real sadness is that it was the presence of the Resident Company which created the historical value of the building, and which engendered the ghostly voices still echoing down to the eager newcomers on both side of the footlights. With the loss of that Company, it is time to pay some tribute to the legacy of its work, some acknowledgement of the debt owed to those who built the original dream, who sustained it over those eighty-six years, and to those actors and audiences who profited from its ethos. An era has passed and now, with some sadness, we let the canvas unfold so that some glimpse of what was the reality within the building may have a visible form to your mind's eye.

*Chapter Two*
## TRADITION AT YOUR BACK

In June 1997, John Franklyn-Robbins wrote, "I remember an actor I am proud to have shared a stage with, storming down the corridor at the Barbican and in rolling tones, exclaiming, 'Ye call this a f★★★ing theatre?' I understand him. It takes years to create 'theatreness' inside a building. But the past and the present are good companions at Liverpool Playhouse. You can feel tradition at your back willing you to go on, to honour those glorious ones whose pain and pleasure and talent rubbed off on the bricks and mortar, so that when you go backstage all your senses come alive – 'This is where I belong!' … I was honoured at Liverpool. The audience was warm and willing, everyone I met, landladies, even casual acquaintances, made it a favourite place for me. An Actor's Place."

The Liverpool Repertory Company itself was begun in 1911 and, following the principles suggested by Annie Horniman, the original founder of the movement begun in Dublin, it was, "a theatre … started largely as a result of amateur enthusiasm, owned by private citizen shareholders, and governed by a Board of Directors who have no professional interest in the theatre" [Goldie]. In Liverpool, it was largely a movement away from the melodramas of the Edwardian period, towards work that reflected the society in which people lived. Exactly what it meant in reality to the audience, is perhaps quaintly summed up by that wonderful Lancastrian playwright, Harold Brighouse, here quoted from the *Liverpool Daily Post*, [30 September 1924]

> "If it be asked what the Repertory movement has moved, the reply is that it has moved plays to the people and people into plays
> … by recognising that the saloon deck view of life was not the only view, and the man in the stokehole lends himself to dramatic
> treatment equally with the man who pays supertax".

The very ordinariness of a community that wants to absorb theatre and see itself reflected within it. Or as many would and still say, that they want a theatre which treats them as intelligent beings. This idea is encapsulated by St John Ervine, another great Liverpool Playwright of the 1920s, when he said to the Playgoer's Circle, in 1923, "… don't come to the theatre and leave your brains in the cloakroom, … rid yourself of prejudice, and you will get something immensely valuable". The desire for a mixture of entertainment which allows for the improvement of the mind via drama and tragedy, local and international, political and sociological was, and still is, the raison d'être of Repertory.

In 1909, such attitudes led to a catalogue of names, including Ronald Jeans, the son of the Managing Director of the *Liverpool Daily Post*, Professor Sir Charles Reilly of the University, Harley Granville Barker the playwright, and many cultured Liverpool families such as the Rathbones and the Muspratts, striving to bring the new plays by the likes of Shaw, Galsworthy, or Ibsen, to Liverpool. Meetings were held and the campaign gained momentum, until the Repertorists had gained sufficient support to be able to run a short season of plays at Kelly's Theatre in Paradise Street. The Repertorists were given active support from the Playgoers' Club, an organisation which existed in Liverpool for many years. On 22 May 1911, the Company was formally registered at Companies House as the Liverpool Repertory Theatre, Limited, with its registered office at Hellewell's Buildings, 3 Harrington Street, Liverpool, the Company house of the newly appointed Company Secretary, Mr Baskerville Simmonds. Under Reilly's chairmanship, they put in a successful bid for the vacant Star Theatre in Williamson Square. Their first director was the 22-year-old Basil Dean and, in the Box Office, a sixteen-year-old by the name of Maud Carpenter.

The opening night at the newly-purchased theatre began with Company member, Aida Jenoure, reciting a poem written for the occasion by John Masefield. The over-subscribed audience, packed into the building, were rapturous in their applause. Then *The Admirable Crichton* by JM Barrie was performed as the opening play.

## The Chair

1911 – 1912 Professor Sir Charles Reilly *The visionary.*

1913 – 1948 Colonel Sir John Shute *After a rocky start, an enduring financial stability.*

1949 – 1961 Lord Cohen of Birkenhead *Redefined play selection in the social climate of post-war Liverpool. The most financially successful Chairperson.*

1961 – 1962 Sir Charles Trustam *Temporary appointment for nine months.*

1962 – 1965 James Rushworth, OBE *Man of vision, controlled the process of rebuilding the site of Number 15 Williamson Square.*

1965 – 1982 Henry Cotton *[The Lord Lieutenant of Merseyside] Initially controlled the growth of short-term contracts for actors and the development of the Theatre Upstairs.*

1982 – 1988 Carl Hawkins *Adventurous writing innovations set against growing external and internal financial instability.*

1988 – 1991 William Fulton *The last true independent chairman, he was innovative in business sponsorship but grossly hindered by local and national funding battles. The repercussions finally hit the beleaguered theatre.*

1991 – 1994 Barry Dale *Set in place by the Official Administrator. He was a Littlewoods' director, on loan as part of the Littlewoods' sponsorship of the struggling Company. For whatever reason, he was conspicuous by his absence. The work was mostly done by his successor.*

1994 – 1997 Malcolm Landau *A long time member of the Board with similar business connections to Littlewoods, but with greater commitment to the Playhouse. A brave man who continued 'fighting the odds' affecting the Company, in spite of his own serious health problems. Handed over to William Fulton for three months in early 1996. Fulton, acting on behalf of the Board, ends the Kenwright era.*

*Certain distinguished people never achieved the position of Chairperson of the Board, but their contributions and long service should not go unrecorded, most notably that of Lord Simey and Elizabeth Christie.*

**The Artistic Directors.** Originally titled Producers, the Artistic Directors were responsible for the artistic policy of the Company. Visiting directors are not included here. The figures in brackets refer to productions which were directed by the Artistic Directors themselves. Out of a total of nearly 2,000 identified productions of plays, 906 were directed by the following resident artistic directors:

1911 – 1913 **Basil Dean** – "Adventurous, interesting, stimulating regime." [Goldie]. Grossly overspent. Theatre nearly closed. He went on to Birmingham Repertory and then to the growing British film industry. (39 known productions)

1913 – 1914 **Laurence Hanray** – retrenchment and reform – a time of transition. "The tide was turned with the first Shakespeare – *Twelfth Night.*" [Goldie]

1914 – 1916 **Madge McIntosh** – Coped with the restraints of the First World War and was supported by the Commonwealth of Actors. Madge McIntosh hired a young William Armstrong as an actor. (31 known productions)

1916 – 1917 **Muriel Pratt and Bridges Adams** – Husband and wife team. Adams' health meant that his better work is recorded from his time at Stratford. Financially unstable box office, again due to the War. Loss of £1,440. [£360,000 in 1998 values]. (Number of productions not recorded)

1917 – 1918 **George Bellamy** – Lasted only a few weeks. **Percy Foster** – Left after 8 months to join the army. **H Lane Bayliff** – Successful attempt to liven up the image. At the suggestion of **Edwin Thompson**, a Board member from 1913 to 1958, the theatre was re-named the Playhouse. Influenza epidemic [1918] hits box office returns during the Ronald Jeans play, *Give and Take,* but otherwise good returns. (Bellamy 3 productions) (Foster 15 known productions) (Bayliff 12 known productions)

1919 – 1920 **Howard Leslie and Jackson Wilcox** – Successful and inspired programme. Shortage of men because of the War. (10 known productions, mostly co-productions)

1920 – 1921 **Jackson Wilcox** – Successful. Critics give *Merchant of Venice* as his pinnacle. (5 known productions)

1921 – 1922 **Nigel Playfair and Stanley Drewitt** – Playfair came from the Lyric, Hammersmith. The first model of the 'absent' director, Drewitt would be his man in Liverpool. Playfair describes the theatre as being a place of education: not a wholly accepted concept in Liverpool at that time. Extensive use of guest appearances did nothing to avert the worst financial disaster thus far; production loss alone was £4,400 [£108,988]. Improved posters did little to attract custom. All financial reserves, built up in the four highly successful post-war years, were used up as the Board fought to save the Company. This period foreshadows some of the problems felt during the Lawton and Kenwright eras. (Playfair 6 productions in 1921) (Drewitt only 1 production under his name)

1922 – 1940 **William Armstrong** – Returning as the Director, he helped to save the theatre, following the 1922 financial crisis. The decision had been made to give the Repertory only one more chance, before closing for good. Armstrong reinstated a permanent Company, which gave the stability needed to save the theatre. Famous for his work with those who later went on to become known as 'The Hollywood crowd' – Cecil Parker, Rex Harrison, Robert Donat, the Redgraves, Harry Andrews and others. (335 productions, many of them as double bills)

1940 – 1942 **Closed by war** – Shute and Maud Carpenter remained in place, but there was no Company Artistic Director at this time.

1942 – 1946 **Home of the Old Vic** – Shute and Carpenter continued to maintain the building for the Repertory Company. Various producers/directors were brought in by the Old Vic Theatre Company who were leasing the Theatre.

Colonel Sir John Shute, Chairman 1913 – 1948.
After a rocky start, an enduring financial stability.

Lord Cohen of Birkenhead, Chairman 1949 – 1961.
Redefined play selection. The most financially
successful Chairperson.

James Rushworth OBE, Chairman 1962 – 1965.
Man of vision, controlled the process of rebuilding
the site of Number 15 Williamson Square.

Henry Cotton, Chairman 1965 – 1982.
Controlled growth of actors' short-term contracts and
the development of the Theatre Upstairs. [Phil Cutts]

Carl Hawkins, Chairman 1982 – 1988.
Adventurous writing innovations set against growing
external and internal financial instability. [Phil Cutts]

William Fulton, Chairman 1988 – 1991.
He was innovative in business sponsorship but
grossly hindered by funding battles. [Phil Cutts]

Certain distinguished people never achieved the position of Chairperson of the Board, but their contributions and
long service should not go unrecorded, most notably that of Lord Simey and Elizabeth Christie.

*Basil Dean, Artistic Director 1911 – 1913.*
*Adventurous, interesting, stimulating regime.*

*William Armstrong, Artistic Director 1922 – 1940.*
*Famous for his work with those who later went on to*
*become known as 'the Hollywood crowd'.*

*John Fernald, Artistic Director 1946 – 1949.*
*Probably had to cope with the meanest ever budget*
*as the post-war austerity bit into theatre resources.*

*Gerald Cross, Artistic Director 1949 – 1951.*
*Took up the post immediately after being a member*
*of the company as an actor.*

*Willard Stoker, Artistic Director 1951 – 1962.*
*His summer revues, written in association with*
*Ronald Settle, are still recalled with affection.*

*David Scase, Artistic Director 1963 – 1967.*
*A quiet, cultured man, who had the ability to give*
*space to actors.*

*Anthony Tuckey, Artistic Director 1969 – 1975.*
*A writer-director who worked well with other*
*directors.*

*Leslie Lawton, Artistic Director 1975 – 1979. An*
*actor-director, a flamboyant and much-publicised*
*well-loved figure.*

**1946 – 1949 John Fernald** – Probably had to cope with the meanest ever budget for production as the post-war austerity bit into the resources of the theatre. However, he provided sufficiently attractive programmes to the then audience to keep them coming. The plays were not necessarily what he wanted to do, but what he needed to do – a predominance of well-established works. He went on to become Head of RADA and retained his association with the Playhouse by his support of the 'Playhouse Scholarship' scheme for RADA graduates. (44 productions)

**1949 – 1951 Gerald Cross** – Became Artistic Director immediately after being a member of the Company as an actor. His work was in the classic tradition. He continued to perform as an actor after his appointment, and is still remembered for his portrayal of Richard II. (31 productions)

**1951 – 1962 Willard Stoker** – A native of Ormskirk, he was seven when he made his first visit to the Playhouse to see *Fifinella* (1914). Later he trained at RADA and in 1951 came to the Playhouse as Artistic Director. He claims that his associations with Tyrone Guthrie and the Playhouse's own William Armstrong, were the two greatest influences on his work. He states that William Armstrong, not long before his death, said to him, "Look after my wee Playhouse for me!" His summer revues, which he himself wrote for the Company, in association with Ronald Settle, are still recalled with affection. (149 productions)

**1962 – 1963 Bernard Hepton** – Also an Actor-Director, who, during his stay, gave an outstanding performance as Sir Thomas More in *A Man for All Seasons.*

Following the retirement of Maud Carpenter, changes in administration severely restricted his freedom as a Director. He is nonetheless still honoured, with great affection, for a stylish programme and for his ideas for accommodating the changing needs of performers in a world increasingly dominated by TV. (11 productions)

**1963 – 1967 David Scase** – A very quiet, cultured man, who was not only a great director but had the ability to give space to those whose acting skill is today universally recognised in current television and films, eg. Anthony Hopkins, Patrick Stewart, Lynda La Plante and many others. If he had one problem whilst at Liverpool, it was having to contend with the upheavals of the redevelopment of the building. (40 productions)

**1967 – 1969 Kay Gardner** – A stopgap appointment from within the Company, who at the time, had the advantage of the opportunities afforded by the completed new building. She had the benefit of an increased box office, brought about by the curiosity of the public wishing to see the new alterations, but when she applied for the permanent post, the Board decision went against her. (7 productions)

**1969 – 1975 Anthony Tuckey** – A Writer-Director who worked well with other directors and who fostered the growth of the innovative Theatre Upstairs by his trusting use of trainees and junior members of staff. He was a very quiet man backstage and retiring in public. His development of trainee directors and his own refusal to lower his standards, has meant that he is still regarded by the Board, theatre staff and many actors with great affection. (53 productions)

**1975 – 1979 Leslie Lawton** – In contrast to Tuckey, Lawton was an Actor-Director, a flamboyant and much-publicised well-loved figure, who brought a different atmosphere to the theatre. He preferred to work with established actors from London, his contacts were wide-ranging and he demanded a more professional marketing approach. Though many audiences loved him, others felt he over publicised himself. There were personnel problems, particulary affecting backstage departments. His style and use of guests mirrors the later 1991 – 1995 period. (29 productions)

*William Gaunt, Artistic Director 1979 – 1981. An actor-director who was introduced to the Liverpool Playhouse as an actor during the Leslie Lawton period. A very different style of production on the main stage and an excellent track record in the Theatre Upstairs.*

**1979 – 1981 William Gaunt** – An Actor-Director who was introduced to Liverpool Playhouse as an actor during the Leslie Lawton period. A very different style of production on the main stage and an excellent track record in the Theatre Upstairs. As a performer, he has since returned to the Playhouse on several occasions. His most memorable, in the first production of *Educating Rita*, when he starred alongside Kate Fitzgerald. (16 productions)

**1981 – 1984 Bill Morrison, Christopher Bond, Alan Bleasdale, Willy Russell** – In an attempt to reintroduce the ethos of new writing into the Playhouse, this team, well-known for its association with the Everyman, was appointed. Morrison retained the longest commitment to the business side of the role of Artistic Director. Affectionately nicknamed 'The Gang of Four,' to the public they still carry a folk memory of innovation and daring. The pressure of running the theatre so impeded their writing opportunities, that each in turn asked to be released from his contract. Nevertheless, this period is renowned for the January 1983 production of *Blood Brothers* and for encouraging many new works by young writers. (Bond 9 productions, 1 co-production) (Bill Morrison 6 productions) (Russell co-directed 2 productions)

**1985 – 1986 Jules Wright** – Described by Helen Chappell in *The Guardian* [23 April 1986] as having had a successful year at the Playhouse. Jules Wright was unhappy at the repercussions from the loss of County Council funding and felt frustrated at both in-house attitudes and the effect of Thatcherite principles generally. She achieved seven new plays in the programme of twelve productions, plus a successful studio season. (9 productions)

**1986 – 1991 and 1991 – 1995 Ian Kellgren** – Took up this position coinciding with the first serious financial ripples from the break-up of Merseyside County Council. His programming immediately returned to a good cross between tradition and innovation and he sought to bring back the long-term subscriber. In this he was ably helped by Roger McCann and David Fishel. By the late 1980s the political climate in the Arts Council, combined with the deteriorating response from the five local authorities, led the Company into a financial impasse. The point was reached in 1990 when the only way forward was to seek a bank loan, to cover contracted commitments. Subsequent failure of promised levels of funding led to the 1991 Administration. (Kellgren 13 productions during 1986 – 1991)

**1991 – 1995 Bill Kenwright [Executive Producer based in London] and Ian Kellgren Artistic Director for the Playhouse** – History will acknowledge Bill Kenwright as the man who offered to rescue the Playhouse. His 'little black book' of well-known actors became a symbol of his style of production. Ian Kellgren remained in place as the Artistic Director to oversee the running of the Playhouse Theatre, until January 1995. Bill Kenwright is also recalled as having started as a boy actor at the Theatre in *The Banbury Nose*, May 1959, and for serving as an ASM. (Kellgren 11 productions 1991 – 1995) (Kenwright 6 productions 1991 – 1995)

**1995 – 1996 Bill Kenwright Executive Producer** – No In-house Artistic Director at this time. Bill Kenwright continued in place for a further fifteen months, with an Administrative Director, Halyna Dyszkant, as his in-house representative/contact. During this period Kenwright did not direct any new productions himself.

**1996 – 1998 Richard Williams** – An experienced Director, familiar with the ethos of repertory, who after careful consideration of the problems surrounding the financial management of this theatre, courageously proposed a return to a full repertory season with a repertory company. The Board accepted his plan and he enjoyed a growing response from the public. The Company closed on the seventh most financially successful year of its entire history. (See Chapter Nine: The Achilles Heel) (13 productions)

'The Gang of Four' 1981 – 1984.
Bill Morrison, Christopher Bond, Alan Bleasdale and Willy Russell – In an attempt to reintroduce the ethos of new writing into the Playhouse, this team, well-known for its association with the Everyman, was appointed.

Ian Kellgren, Artistic Director 1986 – 1991 and 1991 – 1995.
Took up this position coinciding with the first serious financial ripples from the break-up of Merseyside County Council.

Bill Kenwright, Executive Producer based in London, 1991 – 1995.
Executive Producer, 1995 – 1996. History will acknowledge Bill Kenwright as the man who offered to rescue the Playhouse.

Richard Williams, Artistic Director 1996 – 1998.
An experienced Director, familiar with the ethos of repertory.

27

**The Magic of Maud.** Years after she has died, stories of Maud Carpenter still surface in conversation and get passed on to the newcomers. Stephen Boswell, a Company member for two seasons in the seventies, long after Maud had died, wrote in with memories of being told, "There was a board meeting to discuss the next season's plays. 'What about *The Wild Duck*?' someone suggested. 'Gawd no!' exclaimed Maud, 'not another of them bird plays!'"

Almost every actor who had memories of Maud has recorded this anecdote, or similar versions, such as Linda Polan's, "... (Maud), invited to another repertory theatre on the opening night of their production of *Hedda Gabler*, after the curtain calls rose to her feet disgruntledly exclaiming, 'As soon as I heard that shot at the end, I knew I'd seen it before!'"

Harold Goodwin, the account of whose arrival is given in Chapter Three, has another variation of this theme. He describes Maud when, "... she always sat every three weeks at the back of the Stalls, to watch the new production, and she came round afterwards with her choice comments, what she thought about it. And we were doing Ibsen's *The Doll's House* and the final thing in the play is where Nora is leaving her husband and she walks out and you hear the front door slam, and the tabs come down. She came backstage and she said 'Very nice, Eileen (Eileen Herlie), very nice indeed, but you know, as soon as I heard that door slam I knew I'd seen it before!'"

Benjamin Whitrow refers to whatever was Maud's latest gaffe, as being one of the main topics of conversation, whenever the Company was relaxing. One such must have been Caroline Blakiston's memory of Maud returning from her holiday in Venice, "We went down the Grand Canal in a Lagonda!" or, another often quoted, when she showed Rosalie Crutchley to the newly-decorated dressing rooms, "I'm lethargic to paint!" Of such stuff is affectionate memory composed and treasured. Over the years they have become part of the folk lore, the in-jokes of those who belong, the signal that you are worthy of sharing in the verbal traditions of the Company.

Not all the stories are so ingenuous. Indeed there were as many sharp intakes of breath at the mention of her name, as there were affectionate remembrances because, in reality, Maud was feared as much as she was loved and was renowned for getting her own way, even if it meant going directly to the Chief of Police, or higher. Linda Polan's other Maud story has a certain ring of truth about it:

> "... some years later, I met at a social gathering in Liverpool, a man who had been a Magistrate there in her (Maud's) time. He told the story of an actor being brought before his court one day, for ... exposing himself near a public loo in Liverpool City Centre. Just as the bench was about to decide on the poor fellow's fate, Maud rushed into the court, down the aisle and, fearful to lose an actor for that night's performance and probably have to offer a refund, pleaded with the Magistrates, 'Please, Sirs, let him go, I beg you. He merely forgot to put it away!"

Few have quarrelled with this story, but Maud's assistant from the late 1950s, Bill Selby, was not overly keen on this version, believing Maud would have worded it differently.

One has to wonder at the physical and mental agility which could not only control the finances of the daily running of the Company, the discipline of its members and the vagaries of the paying customers, but also find time to lead the Soroptimists, be actively involved in community work, be a regular worshipper in the Anglican Faith, run a household of her own and make time for other people in her busy schedule. A typical comment is from part of Harold Goodwin's tape:

*Maud Carpenter, Playhouse Administrator 1922 – 1962. The unofficial Lady Mayoress of Liverpool.*

*"She was wonderful. She kept things immaculate. She had no artistic ability whatsoever, and ended up as a Director in the Board, but she was a wonderful character, she really was. It took about twelve months for her to speak to me again, and she said, in walking through the stage door, 'How are you getting on?' I said 'Oh, fine, thank you, yes.' She said 'I believe you're married?' 'Yes. Yes I am, yes.' 'Is she an actress?' 'Oh, no, no.' 'Oh, that's a good thing. Yes, a very good thing.' She said 'Well, you must come and have tea with us. Yes, you must bring her, come and have tea. I live on the Wirral, you know, I've got a lovely house, a wonderful house. I've got everything a millionaire's got, only on a smaller scale.'"*

It is fairly obvious that she worked anything up to an eighteen hour day. Her first job came about because as a sixteen-year-old she visited her sister, Blanche, who worked in the Box Office at Kelly's Theatre, Paradise Street. Joining her in this type of work, she became one of the new Company's first employees. She continued in Box Office work at the Rep during its early years.

It could not always have been easy for this Lancashire girl with flat vowels, a rather strange approach to life and a slightly larger than normal height for women at that time. Later her hairdresser of the 1930s, Mrs Nell Fairclough, recalls how Maud had an impressive height and dignity about her and yet had an innocence which was her real charm. A canniness which meant that behind that facade there was an ability to reason out problems and get her own way. The saying of Maud that she remembers hearing the most frequently was, "Nothing great is achieved without enthusiasm."

But perhaps the Colin Voake recording of Ronald Settle's opinion of Maud is the most important one for a deeper insight into the magic of her memory:

**Settle** *Now, Maud Carpenter, that's the one name that you can't possibly separate from the Playhouse. If it hadn't been for Maud Carpenter, I don't think there would have been a Playhouse, as we knew it in those days.*

**Voake** *Why, what was special about her?*

**Settle** *It is very difficult to say. After she died I was asked if I would write the biography of Maud. I knew her very well. Everybody said it's just got to be done. I thought it had, too! So I did go about this and got about half of the material gathered, wrote to various people who'd been in the theatre. I wrote to Tyrone Guthrie, he was in America then. He knew her very well. Well, everybody did, because nobody ever forgot Maud. No matter how good you were, well you could have a name like Guthrie for instance, but you still almost genuflected when you passed Maud. She had this curious effect upon people, no matter who you were: Lord Mayors, they came and went, but Maud Carpenter was still, as somebody once said, 'the unofficial Lady Mayoress of Liverpool.' And she had a terrific influence upon everybody, including those they used to call the producers rather than directors, and they all came under this influence of Maud, who was a most superb, ... well she thought she was a theatre manager, which she was, although she didn't know really anything about theatre, curiously enough. She used to make all sorts of mistakes like she couldn't remember titles of plays. She'd always get mixed up somewhere or other and she'd pronounce them wrongly. In fact, so much of this went on they became known as 'Maudisms'. Years later, people like Cyril Luckham would ask, 'Have you got any more Maudisms?' But she was an enormously influential figure. Many producers have said she had a curious knack of knowing when a play would be a success or not.*

**Voake** *She was the woman in the street, to a certain extent?*

**Settle** *Yes, she was always very well dressed. I don't mean, how shall I put it? I mean for Maud, she always looked elegant, she* *looked like the Queen Mother sort of thing, not overdressed but always looked marvellous. I think Basil Dean put it the best. He said she was the best theatre house manager that the world has ever had.*

**Voake** *He went as far as that?*

**Settle** *Oh yes. Basil and I were very great friends and when he was up in Liverpool, in the latter days, he used to stay with us at home. Yes, the sets had to be nice and the costumes had to be nice, otherwise Maud would have something to say in that curious way. Many people have tried to talk like Maud, and they can't. Impossible! She wasn't common, that's the wrong word to use, but she wasn't an educated woman in the posh way, she used to drop her aitches like mad. Yet she had a great dignity, everybody had something to say about Maud. She ruled them, Lord Cohen even was scared of Maud at times. They all were. Basil, I don't know if he was afraid of her, but he respected her.*

**Voake** *Was this just because she knew her own mind and wasn't afraid to say anything to anybody?*

**Settle** *Yes, to the Playhouse, Maud was exactly what Lillian Bayliss was to the Old Vic. Just like that. A dedication to the theatre which meant the Playhouse came before everything, with Maud. It was just that.*

In her very early years at the theatre, there was an innocence that she herself speaks of, as if wishing to be part of the humour which surrounded her. One day, she was only about eighteen or nineteen at the time, as she recalls in an article in the *Liverpool Echo* [1 November 1961], she approached Basil Dean offering to help him with his clerical work. "As he was concentrating on his rehearsal, without even looking around, the young director said, 'Go to hell!' Peeved by this, I walked out of the theatre and walked home. But, I was back at the theatre that night and when Mr Dean asked me where I'd been, I replied, 'You told me to go to hell, so I went home!' It wasn't until afterwards that it dawned on me why Mr Dean and the rest of the Company roared with laughter.'"

It seems that she came to realise that she could drive hard bargains with men of steel, by allowing them to believe her ingenuous and artless. There are those who have commented that it must have become a useful contrivance or subterfuge, eventually used by her to manipulate her power. There are those who would rather call it an influence for good.

Later, after her death, Mary Ventris writing in the Liverpool Echo of 19 June 1967, speaks of Maud as one, "... who combined the intricate business side of Liverpool Playhouse, where she was General Manager, with the duties of a gracious, welcoming hostess, thus creating an atmosphere in the theatre which one rarely finds elsewhere ... the City is the poorer for her passing ... she had a gift for sizing up character and rarely in my experience of her ... have I known her to be at fault in her judgement. She was a strict disciplinarian where work was concerned, but had the happy knack of seeing the best in people." James Rushworth in his address at her funeral extends these thoughts with "... although a great lady of the theatre for so many years she was never stage struck and her alert, homely common-sense mind and attitude never lost its objectiveness ... she was critical of all inefficiency and bad work and knew unerringly which plays would succeed and which would not, at the Playhouse. Her stand against much modern playwriting was strong in that she could see no point in bad language, immorality or irreligion for its own sake. How right she was!"

Popular accolades surrounded Maud as the years passed and she was a worthy recipient of both an OBE [1954] and an Honorary Degree from The University of Liverpool. The variety of comment about Maud is in some ways a tribute to her ability to be a multi-faceted human being. Anecdotes of Maud are scattered throughout this volume and, with an apology, we know many more have been left out. She is indeed worthy of a biographical volume of her own.

## Chapter Three
## ONE MAN IN HIS TIME PLAYS MANY PARTS

Every year, during August, the new Company of actors would gather to meet each other, to acquaint themselves with the city, to get to know their landladies and to try and uncover for themselves the mystery that made Liverpool Repertory Company one of the most famous in the land. Today, many of these young men and women have universal recognition, but Liverpool knew them when they were unknowns; fearful and, for the most part, inexperienced. As each year has passed, it has added to the legacy of true stories, growing statistics and, on occasion, the whispered anecdotes commonplace within every family unit. Those actors who have been able to respond to the research for this volume clearly appreciated the stability which came from a ten month contract without the Sunday 'hop' to the next venue. Given time to watch more experienced performers; given the freedom from a weekly search for digs; given the opportunity to get to know and understand audience response by being able to compare reaction to differing plays; they look back with some longing to the wonderful days when they belonged to Liverpool.

From the earliest days the stories can only be gleaned from press cuttings, scrap books and the work of Grace Wyndham Goldie. Those early days saw the likes of both Eileen Thorndike [1912 – 1917] and Laurence Hanray [1911 – 1916] as typical company members. Professor Reilly, in *Scaffolding in the Sky*, comments upon the first professional stage appearance of Noel Coward and Gertrude Lawrence in *Hannele*, written by Gerhardt Hauptmann and directed by Basil Dean in 1913. Professor Reilly says of that modest theatrical beginning, that its real significance was that Liverpool would have to endure the gibe that the event passed unnoticed. Nowadays it is much remembered, not least because it acts as an assurance to every star-struck child actor: you can get there, no matter how modest the beginning.

Less of a child actress, more a Playhouse heroine, Estelle Winwood, who lived to be over one hundred and three-years-old and who became a great Hollywood star, is still remembered as the valiant young actress who, in 1914, with the outbreak of World War One and with the Board of Directors already discussing what they saw as an inevitable closure of the Company, overstretched by mortgage debts and production overspend, inspired the famous 'Commonwealth'. Her idea, which she persuaded the producer Madge McIntosh and 90% of the Company to accept, meant a basic wage, a planned repayment of the outstanding debt and, if successful, a share in the profits. It worked and Estelle is fondly remembered as an inspiration for all young enthusiastic thespians who will not walk away from a challenge. Estelle, having appeared in the first production of the Repertory Company, went on to perform in a further 37 productions for the Company.

Members of the Commonwealth also included William Armstrong, at that time a young actor, William Dexter and over a dozen others. Amongst them was AC Rose, who became a Music Hall star who later appeared at a Royal Command Performance. Older Sandpipers will recall him from the frequent posters for the Floral Pavilion, New Brighton: 'Clarkson Rose presents Old Time Music Hall'.

In 1921, trouble brewed when Nigel Playfair operated as the Company Producer from the Lyric Theatre in London. His expensive tastes were characterised by the importing of stars for special half-hour curtain raisers. One such was Mrs Patrick Campbell, who proved unpopular with her outspoken comments on provincial theatres. Following the invitation to William Armstrong to take up the position of Producer at the Playhouse [Artistic Director, as we now call the role], Mrs Patrick Campbell is reported to have declared it madness, since she would have made "… a great actor of you, and now you're throwing away your chance. And you'll be a little man who sits in an office and makes lists" [Goldie page 134]. That he became one of the greatest of the rep's directors proves he

The War 1914 – 1918 Various extracts from programmes of the time

27 December 1915 – The following late members of the Repertory Company are serving with the Colours; Lawrence Anderson, Scott Anderson, Sheil Barry, Richard Coke, Basil Dean, George Dewhurst, Norman McKeown, Victor H Leslie, John H Roberts, Keith Robertson, W Scott Sunderland, Osmund Wilson.

17 April 1916 – Frederick Cooper, Geoffrey Goodhart. Serving with the Colours.

1914 Frank Forbes Robertson: Killed.

1915 Keith Robertson: Killed.

7 October 1916 – In memoriam: Sheil Barry, London regiment, killed in action.

David Scase's 1965 production of 'The Beaux Stratagem' by George Farquhar with Anthony Hopkins as Boniface and Lynda Marchal [later La Plante] as Cherry.

*Opposite* Wyndham Goldie as Charles Stuart Parnell and Ruth Lodge as Kathleen O'Shea, in the 1937 production of 'Parnell' directed by William Armstrong.

was never just a little man. He is remembered by Lord Cohen of Birkenhead as follows:

"... My third visit to the theatre was to the opening play of the 1922 – 1923 season. It was Major Barbara, with Sybil Archdale in the lead, and was William Armstrong's first production here. His company then included many who were to deserve and find wider fame – Herbert Lomas, James Harcourt, Hugh Sinclair, Muriel Aked, Aida Jenoure, Viola Lyel and Muriel Randall ... it was Colonel Sir John Shute who steered this theatrical craft through the dangerous currents and storms of its earlier years, so that by the mid-1920s it had reached smooth waters and was speeding to success." [Press cutting in Archive – undated.]

He does not make any mention of the young Angela Baddeley or her sister Hermione, but one actor from the early 1930s few can forget is Cecil Parker, that master of comedy film from the 1930s to the 1950s, including the film version of *The Admirable Crichton*. Parker appeared in quite a few of the 1920s productions, and is best remembered in Liverpool for his varied character portrayals in twenty-seven Company productions. The best, seemingly, *The Queen's Husband*, *The Inquest*, *The Cathedral*, *Shall We Join the Ladies*, *Cabbages and Kings*, *The Tragedy of Macbeth* and *Lover's Leap*. Cecil's urbane and gracious manner was much commented upon by many who responded to our request for memories of actors. He met and married Muriel Randall during his time at the Playhouse.

Another well-remembered name from this period is that of Lloyd Pearson. His enduring ability to play major and minor roles with equal unaffectedness endeared him to producers and public alike. Others argue that he was frequently no more than a walk-on, minor role actor, just filling in with the 'spear carriers'! But memory clouds, and the records name him in 149 cast lists; the assumption is therefore that he was a valuable member of the Company, whatever the significance of the part played. Like Diana Wynyard, who appeared in 22 productions between 1927 and 1929, Lloyd Pearson was a complete Company member, the type who helped establish the traditions of professional behaviour which characterised Liverpool Repertory from that time onwards.

The 1930s begin the period when programme portraits and production shots became available for most of the shows. Thanks to the industrious Maud Carpenter, we have a visual record of this period, no matter how poor in photographic quality, which is almost complete in company personalities. The companies from this period seem to be composed of many now famous names. The truth must be re-iterated here – that during their time with the Repertory Company, nearly all of the performers had little or no national recognition. Companies were for the large part all unknowns, many straight out of college or university, or star-struck youngsters still in their teens, who worked for a pittance to learn the trade. Many stayed for years, waiting as long as five years to get their photograph in the programme. Suddenly you were 'one of the nobs'! Reflecting upon this period, one cannot help noticing how large some of the casts lists were, in comparison with modern productions – Shaw's *St Joan* [1937] and Elmer Rice's *Street Scene* [1938] each list 47 characters, not counting 'Passers-by'. There is no doubt that many of the young trainees in the pre-war period were happy to fill in the spaces without financial remuneration.

Although many now famous names were often recalled by older Liverpool ladies, less well known names would also quite suddenly, and with obvious affection, be remembered as their heroes from that time. One popular late 1930s name is that of the dashingly handsome Roderick Lovell. In March 1938, Joyce Owen and 15 school friends came to see *Jane Eyre*. Roderick Lovell played Mr Rochester. Joyce paid 2/4d for a seat in the Pit Stalls and returned twice more, the third time having to stand at the back of the theatre.

*The 1936 Staff Outing. Maud Carpenter is next to the coach with the 14-year-old Stanley Williams. Doris Houlton is front row left, wearing a diamond patterned dress. [Stanley Williams' collection]*

One lovely memory of Robert Donat [above] and Cecil Parker came from 91-year-old Phyllis Coates. As an 18-year-old starstruck teenager working in town as a milliner, she would spend many of her lunch breaks at a cafe called 'Rest a While', waiting for her idols to come in for their sandwiches and coffee. She said she could believe the stories of how Maud made them all dress smartly and behave graciously. She spoke of the image of them standing back to let ladies pass and how she knew that other girls would try to get to the door in time for the privilege of the actors holding open the door for them, doffing their hats and giving a slight bow. She believed them to be very modest men. Over the years her favourites remained as Donat, Flemying, Edwards, Sangster and Redgrave. Phyllis also recalled that she and her friend would watch the stage door in Houghton Street, but never once did they dare approach one of the actors to speak to them. Happy to queue for the gallery, she did sometimes save 1/4d for a Pit Stalls seat as she got a little older. By then she was also lunching at Cooper's, sitting in the balcony area with her new boyfriend!

Mrs Marjorie Graham, who in the 1930s worked in Hanover Street, remembers the 1933 production of *Dear Brutus* and has fond memories of William Armstrong; as well as some of the less frequently mentioned. She described Marjorie Fielding as a motherly type and Robert Flemyng as flamboyant. Wyndham Goldie she described as well-built and powerful, wonderful in *Parnell* and with a smile said, "I was quite turned on by the manly Stephen Jack," and loved the elegance of Ena Burrill and Judy Campbell. Marjorie spoke of her speculations as to which actor would get which role and her disappointment if favourites were not cast in the best parts. Her especial memories were of the last night of each season. Booked since the January, the planning of new dresses and hairstyles kept the excitement going until, on the night, they frequently had the pleasure of receiving a flower from an actress's bouquet. In 1956 Mrs Graham, along with many others, mourned the death of Marjorie Fielding who had described her seven years with the Company as some of the happiest years of her life and during which time she had played nearly a hundred parts.

Local boys, Deryck Guyler and Rex Harrison, were at school together and both joined the Playhouse company in the 1930s, although not in the same season. As Mrs Audrey Roper and many other ladies remember, Harrrison was christened 'Sexy Rexy' by his devoted fans; they were delighted (and perhaps a little surprised) when much later he became Sir Rex.

Hollywood gave Robert Donat universal recognition and acclaim, but his stay at the Playhouse from 1928 to 1930 and his retention of a coastal home near Liverpool, gave him an especial place in local people's affections. Living memories of Robert are now few and far between, but his name will always be remembered, not least because, on the occasion of the Centenary [1996] of Cinema, the Brirish Film Institute presented a plaque in recognition of his early performances at the theatre. The plaque also records the work of Rex Harrison and Michael Redgrave.

Geoffrey Edwards (1931 – 1935) was a repertory actor of outstanding skill and his greatest performance was as Hamlet, which he played just before making his West End appearance in Priestley's *Duet in Floodlight*. Priestley was so impressed that he wrote a part specially for him in *Spring Tide*. After appearing in two further Priestley plays, Geoffrey became entitled to wear the famous Priestley Club tie.

**The day War broke out.** Judy Campbell was a Company Member in 1939. Now in her eighties and still in touch with Rachel Gurney, the tape of her memories, sent in response to a letter from the author, is so colourful that a large section of the transcription is given almost verbatim. Quite apart from the images of 1939 Britain, she shares with us some of her vivid memories of Deryk Guyler and William Armstrong. The honesty and warmth of Judy's tape, her voice still clear and vibrant, is the author's favourite of all the tapes now kept in the Archive.

*"My memories of Liverpool are cut in half by the War. I also remember the grandeur of it compared with the weekly Rep that I'd been in at £3 a week, on and off for two years ... playing leading parts in dresses that had belonged to friends of my mother, which had been wildly cut down and pinned up with safety pins, and only a week allowed for rehearsal. Then I went on a long tour with Vic Oliver and Sarah Churchill in a play called 'Idiot's Delight'. And when we got to Liverpool we all stayed, I can't believe I stayed, at the Adelphi! I still wasn't getting very much compared with Vic. We went to a party at the Adelphi, a supper party, and there was William Armstrong, who unhesitatingly made for our table and asked me how I felt about coming up the following season to be the leading lady. I'd always heard you'd needed a blood test to get into Liverpool, rather than an audition*

*Deryck Guyler as Baron Appenschlappenelitz in 'It Might Happen to You'.*

*James Stephenson. [Stanley Williams' collection]*

*Geoffrey Edwards.*

**Opposite** *Believed to be 'Hobson's Choice' by Harold Brighouse [1926] It is the earliest surviving photograph in the Liverpool Repertory archive and shows Doreen Moss, Constance Pelissier, Gerald Pemberton, Muriel Randall and Cecil Parker.*

William Armstrong as the melancholy Jacques in 'As You Like It' 1946 directed by himself.

**Opposite** Rachel Gurney and Peter Robinson in 'The Anatomist' by James Bridie, 1938 directed by Charles Thomas.

and we'd asked if he'd seen the play, and no, he hadn't! But I was wearing a rather smashing dress and he had no hesitation. Vic made me argue about salary and said I must get twelve … and when I went to see William, he said he never paid twelve, he never paid more than ten! However, I won and I remember soon after, I gave an interview, some newspaper or other, and I said what I was earning and when I got to the theatre there were fearful dramas taking place and William had taken to his chaise longue, in the theatre, in his room there, and he said, lying under his fur rug, 'How could you do it to me? How could you do it? Alfred Sangster only gets ten and I lied about you!' I think he kept to his bed for about three days. I loved William … David Webster was very much in evidence, he was still running Lewis's, I think, and they used to lend us dresses and David would invite one back. As you know he later became administrator of Covent Garden, but all the records he played to us were of American musicals: Hart and Rodgers … oh, I remember all those songs, even now, and sitting in that big room of David's with his splendid gramophone and listening to these very sophisticated American songs for the first time.

The first play I did was 'Arms and the Man' with Bill Mervyn, oh such a joy to act with, he played Bluntschli, the Chocolate Soldier, and Edward Sinclair played Sergius, the dashing Hussar. The second play was … oh lovely … 'Reunion in Vienna', originally written for the Lunts [Alfred Lunt and Lynne Fontanne]: a marvellous part for me, and Edward Sinclair played the Alfred Lunt part of the ex-princely one, now a taxi driver, who comes back to Vienna … and Deryck Guyler played my husband. And he was a joy to work with too. I'm trying to get names right…

When war was declared, we were doing a new play called 'Spears Against Us'. It was adapted from the novel and the irony of it was, it was all about an aristocratic Austrian family in the fourteen-eighteen war. I played Paula von something or other and ended up, when Germany lost the war, as a prostitute who was discovered by someone in a brothel. Whereas to begin with we had all been playing tennis on a beautiful sunny day in 1914. And outside the newspaper boys were shouting, 'Hitler going into Poland!' So, it was very odd because you could sense the feeling in the street outside. And that night, some of the company came back to my flat, I had a flat in Huskisson Street, next door to William [Armstrong] and William came back, several members of the company and Bobby [Robert] Helpmann and a couple of other people from the Ballet which was up there and Bobby did his imitations to cheer us all up and I played my gramophone and he sang Mary Ellis' 'My Rapturous Glamorous Nights' and he dressed up in my evening dresses. I had a great wardrobe of evening dresses because of the sort of plays we did. Bobby dressed up in my black satin with the sequins, he dressed up in my white chiffon which I'd worn in 'Reunion in Vienna'. Oh, he dressed up in five or six of my dresses, seizing on them excitedly, going into the bathroom and coming out flinging my first night flowers all around the room. William sat over the gramophone, he also played some Yvonne Printemps records I had, and he sat crying and saying that he was going to sit out the war in the Hebrides, if his friend McPhee would have him, and he was just going to take his objets d'art and not be seen again until the war was over. And he was weeping and saying, 'The lights were going out all over Europe and we would not see them lit in our lifetime again'. And underneath we all felt a curious bewildered excitement, not exactly a pleasurable excitement, but a sort of dread. It was a rather marvellous party. The next morning I woke up to find a note from the landlady, she was going to sit the war out in Luton, I think! I remember making myself some porridge and hearing that phoney air-raid. I recall hearing Mr Chamberlain saying we were at war and there was my flat covered in dead chrysanthemums and roses, evening dresses draped around the sofa and chairs. We saw the immense queues at the railway

station, so four of us clubbed together and bought a car, a Ford V8 I think! We paid eight pounds for it because it ate up petrol. We paid two pounds each. I was dropped off first in Lincolnshire, in Grantham where my parents lived, and the others continued on down. David Dobell, I think it was, and Nicky Bruce (he played my fiancé in 'Spears Against Us') – anyway, I stopped off at Grantham and had vague ideas that I would probably be driving an ambulance across France because all one's ideas were based on what one had heard about the 1914 – 1918 War, so I thought that clearly this was what I was going to do. And then, two or three weeks went by, and a postcard arrived from William saying he was back in Liverpool and he thought we'd better start again, doing very small plays in very small sets. Oh, and we all gathered up there, indeed doing very small plays in very small sets, and then before Christmas the cast decided to put on a revue, and it was going to be – the contents of this revue – a secret from William. I think it was mostly written by Alfred Francis, who was trying to establish the 'Late Joys' in Liverpool and was a very happy man. Some of the young men had joined up right away, I'm sure Nicky Bruce did, so he wasn't in the revue but I did sometimes see him. His mother was [the ballet dancer] Karsavina; I think she came up with Fred [Sir Frederick] Ashton to see 'Spears Against Us'. To meet her was fantastic and wonderful. Anyway, to get back to the revue, Deryck Guyler was in it and he astonished us by playing the washboard; he had thimbles on his fingers and he did a rhythm on the washboard and sang songs he'd made up himself. He was absolutely fantastic, and he was local, so he brought the house down. I had a number about a beautiful spy and I made, or somebody made for me, on the sewing machine – Maud Carpenter was very helpful over it all – a scarlet dress with a feathered thing on my head, sort of looked like Mata Hari, and I was someone or the other, Olga Popovsky, the beautiful spy.

All sorts of people were up in Liverpool, because there was a great to-ing and fro-ing because of the war. Keith Winter was up there on his way to Hollywood to write 'The Red Shoes' and there was a strained air about him, because he didn't want people to think he was going there to escape the war. And so, I think he felt the terrible pull that he ought in a way to stay, but he'd said that he would come back as soon as his age group was called up. In the meantime, he took us to Morecambe Bay to eat shrimps and lots of things. It was lovely; I made a great friend of Keith. He was waiting for a boat and other people were arriving on boats.

My great, great friend was Jenny Nicholson, a trained dancer, the granddaughter of Sir William Nicholson who had taught Sir Winston Churchill to paint. It was through her that Sarah Churchill had been allowed to go to the same dancing class as William Nicholson's granddaughter, and then to become a Cochrane Young Lady, and then to meet Vic Oliver, so thereby hangs a great tale. Anyway, Sarah had been a great friend and so Jenny became a great friend, and she really behaved outrageously. At night after the play she'd say 'Let's go to the Adelphi' and I'd say 'Jenny, we can't possibly afford it, we've got to go to the Bide-a-Wee. The Bide-a-Wee was a cafe that was really called the Rest-a-While. Jenny said 'Oh, well. we might meet somebody who'll treat us.' and I thought this was outrageous, but Jenny had a will of iron, and she bent me to her will, and we used to go to the Adelphi, where she would spot any celebrity who had either just arrived on a ship or was waiting for a boat to take them to America, and would brazenly go up to them with her gas mask in its cardboard box and say 'Would you sign my gas mask, it's such a thrill to meet you, and I think I may have met you before, because my father's Robert Graves and my uncle's Charles Bishop.' She was quite shameless about it, and very, very funny, and everybody was delighted to sign her gas mask. Nobody signed my gas mask.

Judy Campbell.

**Opposite** 'Spears Against Us', 1939, directed by William Armstrong. This was the production on stage the day the Second World War was declared. It was closed after only four days. This is the only photograph of that show, taken during the final dress rehearsal, and shows left to right: Jean Brocklebank, Joy Frankam, Judy Campbell, David Dobell, Kenneth Morgan, Guy Verney, Geoffrey Gomer, Susan Richards, Jenny Nicholson, and Charles Percy.

## A. R. P.

Should an Air Raid Warning be given during the performance the audience will be notified from the Stage. Members of the audience will then have the opportunity of either remaining in their seats or taking advantage of the Air Raid Shelter in Messrs. George Henry Lee's basement . . . the entrance is opposite the Stage Door of the Theatre. The Directors of The Playhouse wish to express their appreciation of Messrs. G. H. Lee's generous help in this matter. When the "All Clear" Signal is given and the audience again seated then the performance will be resumed.

*Jenny's gas mask cardboard box was absolutely covered in celebrities. And anyway, Jenny came into her own with the revue ('Repertory Rations', November 1939) because she'd been a Cochrane Young Lady and had beautiful legs and could tap-dance as well. She did a top hat, white tie and tails number that was also an enormous success. So I always remember this revue.*

*Oh, another person who was up in Liverpool was Eric Maschwitz, who already, because of his Polish blood, had leapt into uniform, and he came to see the revue and offered me a job in London, and as I'd already got an agent who'd found me a job in a movie, I left Liverpool shortly afterwards and went into 'New Faces' and sang 'A Nightingale Sang in Berkeley Square' and never went back to Liverpool, so that's really another story.*

*But anyway, to get back to the revue, Jenny had friends in Liverpool who ran one of the Liverpool papers. I went to a luncheon party at the Adelphi, as usual with William, and there we were met by a copy of the newspaper with the headline 'Revue to stay owing to popular demand'. Jenny had fixed it all with her friend that there was to be this cry for the revue to be kept on, and William had not expected this. He'd been very pleased with the revue, but he didn't want it kept on, he wanted to do something else. And so he was furious. I always remember walking round behind the potted palms, with William in tears saying 'She wouldn't have done it to Basil Dean!' Basil Dean was that almost sadistic producer of legendary fame, who made actresses cry! Other memories of William I treasure? William nodding off during rehearsal and waking up with a start and saying 'Oh, I'd have been a great actress if I'd lived!' William taking to his bed before 'Reunion in Vienna' and giving me a little box as a first night present, that came from Sacher's because Sacher came into the play and it was a Sachertorte box with little chocolates inside. I think that's all I can tell you. My time at Liverpool was full of laughter and tears."*

There is no consistent mention, in programmes, of the wartime activity of Company members during the Second World War. This is probably due to the rationing of paper for programmes. Similarly the War and post-war austerity meant that once again publicity photographs were seldom taken at the theatre. It is not until the mid 1950s and early 1960s that we see some return to a pictorial record.

The first indication of war, in the programmes, is during *Lot's Wife* by Peter Blackmore on 28 September 1939, where the comment is made that, "Under present conditions, the producer thought it advisable to curtail, as far as possible, the realism of the volcanic eruption at the end of Act I." Few complete wartime programmes still exist, but on the inside cover of the *Swiss Family Robinson* programme of 23 December 1939 we find an ARP (Air Raid Precautions) notice. This is the earliest example currently in the archive. One anecdote concerning the Second World War is told by Walter George in the volume entitled *The Playhouse, a Review of the Theatre since 1946*. He recounts:

*"Robert Flemyng, a great favourite in the pre-war Playhouse Company, was acting in this play in New York (alongside Lawrence Olivier) when war was declared … When it became apparent that we would soon be at war, Bobby left too. He loved his part, he loved being in New York, he loved playing Kit. But he felt he must go home and enlist. He had a varicose vein in his leg which he knew would disqualify him. So he quit the play and went into the New York Hospital to have an operation on his leg. He sailed for home, qualified for enlistment, and served all through the war. He put in what the English describe as 'a good war'.*

Flemyng was born in Liverpool and began acting in 1931. Later, in his old age, he became President of Liverpool Repertory Company.

Michael Redgrave and Rachel Kempson.

**Opposite** ARP warning from 1939 programme.

Robert Flemyng who went on to became President of the Liverpool Repertory Theatre Company.

**The Old Vic at the Playhouse.** Due to wartime conditions and the anticipated heavy bombing of Liverpool, the Company was disbanded on 15 June 1940. However, in the programme of 2 April 1940, fifteen names, including Robert Flemyng and Peter Neil, are listed as serving in the Forces. There were no productions until 4 November 1942 when the London Old Vic Company became resident in the theatre.

Maud Carpenter and a fire officer spent many nights fire-watching on the roof of the Playhouse until, in 1942, the Old Vic Company was re-housed from its own bomb-damaged London premises. Thus we find in November 1942, Bernard Miles as Iago, followed by an appearance of Lewis Casson as a Ist Chorus in *Jacob's Ladder*, then in *Queen Bee* [1943] Sybil Thorndike as Lady Beatrice Cuff. That same year saw a Michael Redgrave production of the Peter Ustinov play *Blow Your Own Trumpet*, and an Alec Guiness adaptation of *Great Expectations* with Lally Bowers as Miss Haversham. Lally stayed on for several more productions, including *A Doll's House* by Henrik Ibsen, in which she starred as Nora Helmer.

1944 saw the arrival of Ronald Settle and, later that year, Cyril Luckham. Both were to play an enormous part in the successful rebuilding of post-war theatre life in Liverpool, staying on with the Rep Company when the Old Vic went back to London.

Occasionally it can happen that the personality of a particular actor stamps itself on a permanent company, without the wish or conscious effort of that actor. Such a case is Cyril Luckham, who became an institution during his several years at the Playhouse, so much so that it was as hard for him to leave as it was for the audience to let him go. Even now, the 1940s and 1950s are referred to, by those who remember that time, as 'the Luckham era'.

Notable for the variety of roles he played, large and small, taking part in 76 different productions for the Repertory company after an unrecorded number of performances for the Old Vic in 1944 – 1945, his persona was always gentlemanly and amiable, inspiring great affection in his many fans. Prepared to fit in and accept various character roles, he later seemed to be given more of the comedy parts. Mrs Gertrude Usher, a committee member of the Playhouse Circle and the Liverpool Playgoers' Club and also a judge for the British Drama League, believed that he was in danger of getting trapped into emphasising the comedy aspect of any role. After leaving the Playhouse however, in his subsequent stage, film and TV career he was in demand as a portrayer of peers or elderly statesmen, sedate and serious. He is still occasionally observed in repeats of old footage.

We are grateful to Susan Withers' daughter for the loan of the Imelda Campey collection of programmes and photographs. Imelda was his greatest fan and maintained contact with him until his death in 1989. Many others responded in the same vein as Mrs M Roberts of Newcastle under Lyme, Staffordshire, who said of him, "He had the most distinctive voice, I can still hear it today!" Tony Hebbert who, like many other members of the regular audience, used to head for Exchange Station as quickly as possible after the end of the show, was often surprised to find Cyril, changed out of costume and with not a trace of stage make-up, already sitting on the train and reading a paper as though he had been there for hours.

Luckham is here reviewed as 'Popkins' in *Rookery Nook*. As if trying to match Luckham's jest, it is described with some archaic, tongue-in-cheek witticism by the late, and many would say, great, Sidney Jeffery of the *Liverpool Daily Post*:

*"Then – Cyril Luckham! His mesmeric admixture of waywardness with chivalry, as Gerald Popkins, is achieved with brilliant blandishment: While Manning Wilson, as his cousin Clive, would seem nearly as naughty except for his handicap of bachelorhood. Mr Luckham's ladykilling enterprise, ridiculous simper, and uninhibited technique in the sofa approach, reveal*

*Cyril Luckham photographed in 1951. [Courtesy of Imelda Campey]*

*sensational new facets of his art. All this set against, Peggy Mount … the daily dragon whose fiery breath of tittle-tattle lights a forest fire."*

Jeffery's reviews were often of a deep and interesting nature but, on this occasion, the fascinating combination of Luckham, Wilson and Peggy Mount, in full romp, obviously got the better of him.

When he visited Liverpool in March 1973, Cyril Luckham told Lynda Roughley of the *Liverpool Daily Post*, "The decision to leave Liverpool Playhouse broke my heart". Apart from stage work, he had also been greatly involved in the off-stage life of the Company, for example captaining the Playhouse cricket team which played charity matches against teams such as Upton on the Wirral.

A production of Shaw's *Pygmalion* on television in 1956 reunited Cyril Luckham, as Colonel Pickering, with Gladys Boot, as Mrs Higgins. She had been a leading lady of the Playhouse company, sometimes unbending but often elegant and stately in the style of the times and she too went on to success in radio, television and the West End theatre. The *Personalia* column in 1950s programmes was always avidly scanned by fans for news of the activities of former Company members. There are many examples of people's careers parting and meeting again; one item in 1955 reports that Gladys Boot, Brian Oulton and Edward Mulhare were all appearing in a new play, *The Night of the Ball*, at the New Theatre, London.

**The New Wave Actor arrives at the Theatre.** Harold Goodwin (1947 – 1949) describes his introduction to the theatre in an excerpt, transcribed verbatim, from his 1997 taped reply to our request for his memories of his time at the Playhouse:

*"My name is Harold Goodwin. I was born in Yorkshire, I went to school in Manchester. I am eighty years old and retired at seventy-eight. In 1945, I won a scholarship to the RADA, and in 1946 John Fernald came to direct us in a Restoration play, 'The Provoked Wife'. He left to go to be Artistic Director at Liverpool Rep, the number one rep in the country, and one year later, out of the blue, he wrote to me and offered me a 44-week contract at £10 per week [£220 a week at 1998 value]. I was in heaven. A working class northern lad, working in the great Liverpool Rep. We lived in Finsbury Park. I was married to Beatrice. We had very little money, so we decided to go up to Liverpool on the midnight bus so that we could save. We went up and I think the fare was about 22 shillings single. [approximately £24 in the 1998 equivalent]. We arrived in Liverpool and it was pissing down with rain, it looked as if it was never going to stop. Round about eight o'clock in the morning we walked around and had a cup of tea, and later on when Liverpool became alive, at about nine o'clock, she said she [Beatrice] would go to try and find a flat, and I would go down to the theatre.*

*So I got down to the theatre and I was wringing wet, and I went to the Stage Door and the stage door keeper came to me and said 'What do you want?' I said 'Er … I've … I've come to work here.' He says 'What?' I said ' Er … I've come to work here. I want to see Mr Fernald.' 'Oh', he says, 'you can't see Mr Fernald, I mean he's directing at the moment, you can't see him.' 'Well, who can I see?' 'Well, I'd better take you up to Miss Carpenter, she's the General Manager.' So I went up two flights of stairs, still dripping wet, he knocked on the door, opened the door and said 'Oh, Miss Carpenter, there's a man 'ere who wants to work 'ere,' and shut the door. There I was, facing a monumental Maud Carpenter. She looked me up and down and said 'What do you want?' I said 'Er … well … er … I've come to work here.' She said 'What sort of … what's your name … work?' I said 'Well … I've … er, come to work with Mr Fernald.' 'Oh no,' she said, 'We've got our own.' I said 'I beg your pardon?'*

Gerald Harper began as a rep member in 1948 and has the longest performing association with the Playhouse, whereas Cyril Luckham holds the record from the 1940s and 1950s for the greatest number of roles played.

**Opposite** The 1948 production of 'The Silver Curlew' with Peggy Mount, Cyril Luckham, Harold Goodwin. It was directed by John Fernald. The photograph also illustrates the poverty of set material available during the post war period. [Burrell and Hardman]

Terence Knapp.

William Lucas.

**Opposite** 'The Londonderry Heir' [1958] written by Willard Stoker and Ronald Settle – the cast seen in this shot are; John Stride, Patricia Routledge, Jacobus Jacobs, Gwen Williams, Trevor Danby, Caroline Blakiston, Valerie Miller, Thelma Barlow, Terence Knapp, John Gay. Producer Willard Stoker. Design: Alan Pikford. [Loaned by Bill Selby]

*She said 'We've got our own. We've got our own, you see. We don't … I tell you what you should do, you should go to the Royal Court. You see, they pick the stage hands up ad lib, you know.' I thought 'She thinks I'm a stage hand!' I said 'I'm an actor.' She said 'What?' I said 'I'm an actor!' She said, 'Oh, an actor! Oh, I'll take you down to see Mr Fernald then,' and we went down. It wasn't until years later I thought, 'Oh, yes, Maud had never met a New Wave actor, this was the first New Wave actor she had ever seen. [New Wave was a post war, more naturalistic, style of acting which included a move away from the constant use of received pronunciation.]*

*I was then introduced to the Company. There were sixteen in the Company, very large for a rep, and we did a three-weekly. There was three weekly rehearsal and then played three weekly, and the leading man was Cyril Luckham, who was on £30 a week in 1946 – that is about £600 a week now. Dorothy Reynolds was on £25 a week as the leading lady, and she went to London and she wrote the book of 'Salad Days', she was quite famous. It was a wonderful time. We used to do Shakespeare, Shaw, Ibsen, Chekhov and all those plays, and I was learning all the time. And all the time the other members of the company, who were far in advance of me, used to tell me what I should do and what I shouldn't do. That's when I was learning my craft. In RADA you just learn the rules, and now I was learning 'it' and I learnt it for three years and it was the most wonderful experience. When I was coming to London, John Fernald was also leaving and going to the Arts (Theatre), and we went down together, because I was going to be working with him again. He said 'You know, during the last three years that I worked there, there was no Arts Council, there was no subsidy, and do you know, we made a £12,000 profit in the first year, we made £10,000 profit in the second year and we made £8,000 profit in the third year.*

*It was a wonderful, wonderful experience, and all I can say is, that I owe my whole life to the Liverpool Rep and to John Fernald. Thank you!"*

From this period, the actor, Nicholas Amer, is remembered by the then 13-year-old Anthony Higginson as having been very kind to him and to other teenagers appearing in *The Whirligig of Time* in 1949. Nicholas was very young himself in 1949, and a very friendly person: he was one of the few whom members of the audience would dare to speak to, over their pre-performance cheese-on-toast at the Kardomah, Basnett Street. Later, both actors were invited to return for another season. Nicholas in 1980, Anthony Higginson in 1968, when Kay Gardner asked him to stay for over a year, having meanwhile been a fellow-student of Harvey Ashby at RADA in John Fernald's time there.

Peggy Mount appeared in several productions from August 1950 onwards, overlapping the time a young Beryl Bainbridge worked at the theatre. Peggy returned in the seventies, by now a famous theatre and television personality, and still "… filling the air with her deep resonant voice. It seemed to bounce off the walls." [Remembered by Miss Brenda Harris]

Enthusiastic reviews seemed to follow whenever William Lucas was on stage. He was in the 1953 – 1954 company and returned in 1975 and 1977. As with Robert James (see below), so with Lucas, he was a good and well-loved Company member, who seems to be typical of many of the 1950s performers – prepared to put the Company first and 'fit in', rather than make ripples. At that time, a less well known Patricia Routledge worked her way through the training ground of *The Atom Doctor* by Eric Linklater, *The Petshop* by William Chetham, *The Druids Circle*, by John van Druten, and several others. Andrew Sachs was working as the Stage Manager at the time and Patricia was one of two student ASM's for whom he was responsible. He speaks of his admiration for her singing

Gwen Williams on the right, in 'Jeannie' directed by
Willard Stoker, 1958.

**Opposite** Moray Watson and Jill Fenson.

Ann Davies and Brian Bedford.

Mona Bruce and Robert James.

voice and the fact that Patricia still introduces him with, "I swept the stage for him". Without any apparent fuss and seemingly effortlessly, she was discovered as a talented actress and her rise was more meteoric than Andrew's at that period. Sachs left in 1953, when Willard Stoker had insisted upon his continuing to be Stage Manager with no promise of more challenging parts.

[In Sidney Jeffery's journals we find: "In July 1952 Patricia Routledge joined Playhouse Company as a student. Daughter of Mr and Mrs Edgar Routledge of Higher Bebington. Birkenhead High School actress, leaving in July 1947 for Liverpool University, where she graduated in English language and literature, and was a leading member of the University Dramatic Society. In six months she became a junior member of the Playhouse Company … and [after five productions] went to Bristol Old Vic in musical plays."]

Again the use of local writers began to be observed as a pulling power in the box office. Gwen Larwood of St Katherine's Training College, Childwall, had her first full length play, *The House of Benedicite*, accepted for production. It attracted Charles Carson into the lead role and in spite of being programmed against a Royal Court production of *The Lark*, with Dorothy Tutin in the lead, it held its own and is still remembered with enthusiasm by many Liverpool people. It helps us understand why, when we see the cast list: Ann Davies, Terence Knapp, Margaret Diamond, Andrew Sachs, Jill Fenson, Gwen Williams, Charles Carson, Robert James, Brian Peck, William Roderick, Anthony Service, Moray Watson, William Fry.

In his written notes on *The House of Benedicite*, Sidney Jeffery writes, "Stoker handled all with a keen eye for detail". Willard Stoker was, as Artistic Director of the Company, also aware of people's need to try out new skills. As such, he gave opportunity to Robert James to work as a director, sometimes assisting himself and sometimes allowing him the full weight of the responsibility. It proved an excellent opportunity for Robert, remembered as one of the best Company members. Richard Briers adds to that memory in a transcript from part of a taped interview with Colin Voake:

*"Robert James? A great Company member – he directed sometimes and gave Ann [Davies, Brier's wife] her first acting part in 'Beauty and the Beast'. I always felt his genuine modesty held him back. He held that Company together, he was consistent. He held everything together and was a blessing to Bill Stoker. He was a genuinely nice man. Very caring about the company. I think he cared more for the Playhouse than he did for himself. Mona Bruce [Robert's wife] backed Robert, she was a genuine person as well."*

Richard Briers' tape is full of interesting comment. A substantial amount is reproduced here, because it reflects many of the more universal feelings and aspects of conflict or opportunity, common to many a beginner's year in a company:

*"… I was terrified, because in those days the first repertory engagement was absolutely amazing. I'd got the scholarship to Liverpool having just completed 'Hamlet', in the main role at RADA, to find myself in Brian Bedford's 'Hamlet' as a priest and a soldier and a third or fourth player … A demotion! But, I knew I'd get a lead sometime. I was flat broke and earning £8.00 a week … I remember … 'School for Wives' … so nervous I could not eat a thing and Terry Knapp was trying to make me eat a steak. I was nervous, and was so for many years. I used to be quite sick before performing. I'm over it now, but then it was every time. It was very romantic in those days, … it sounds pretentious now, but you went to conquer a city … you'd arrive in Liverpool and you must shine as an actor! In those days to get to Liverpool Rep was quite an honour and it was three weekly rep, which was regarded as a step up from the fortnightly and weekly shows. It was a big date to one so young – I was a very young 22-year-old.*

… Elmer Rice came over for his play, 'Dream Girl', and for Pauline Yates it was a big opportunity, later he would offer her a place in New York but the Playhouse wouldn't release her from her contract to let her go … she went to Maud and got told, 'Well, you don't really want to go to Broadway, do you?' … After Liverpool – it was unthinkable to Maud. Liverpool was the centre of the world!

… I was very anxious when I was with Maud as she had a way of looking at you – a sort of pressing you, in a way. I thought I should get ten pounds a week … I was apologetic … she looked at me and said, 'Well, you get the best parts, don't you? Well, that's all you need to worry about, then. You'll make more money when you leave here.' She was right really!

… Willard Stoker loved musicals and was very good at them. I didn't realise how good he was until I left there. He loved comedy. He encouraged me and became a great friend.

… Pauline Yates – she did mostly light comedy parts. She had a very dry sense of humour – never overplayed her part – a nice company member, a real delight to work with.

… Gwen Williams could be quite frightening. Very competent. She must have been quite old even then. You always called her Miss Williams. There was no Tannoy in those days so we had to run round knocking on the doors. If it was your turn to call, she used to be angry if you didn't wait for her to say thank you. She'd make such a fuss about it, but it taught you a lesson, not to assume that she'd been in her room and heard you. You had to be certain that everyone was safely on stage in good time. That was a very good lesson. Robert James was a good friend to her. She could be very sweet and help people like Ann to do her hair. She told a story which showed how tough it could be, during the 1914 – 1918 War, she was on stage, in a crowd scene, when she suddenly spotted her brother in the audience. He was back from France, sitting there in his uniform. She was so happy that she smiled at him. But this was noticed and she was suspended, told off in front of all the Company.

… William Roderick, a complex man, handsome and eccentric. A truly remarkable stage presence.

… Helen Lindsay? Delightful. Very intense and dramatic, great stature, my height – she acts six foot tall. Great presence.

… Terence Knapp, one of the RADA students, two years before, I think! Scored a big hit in one of the St John Ervine plays. He now teaches in Hawaii as a professor of drama.

… Brian Bedford, another scholarship boy. He had the most incredible wish to succeed, sex appeal, energy and a very fine actor. He became a star in America.

… 'The Apple Cart' … Sets by Alan Pikford, very talented. Married Helen Lindsay.

… I remember Sue Withers was there for years and years. I remember her and May Finch who worked with her. Sue ruled the wardrobe with a rod of iron.

… Thelma Barlow came for 'The Glass Menagerie', yes, she came up for it. The first thing she did with the company and then she stayed on for quite some time. Excellent production!

… Mr Potter? Me playing an 80-year-old man living abroad – I had to wear gloves to disguise my young hands. I played old men well, so I got a little type cast, but I don't mind. It was Ann's favourite role for me!

… 'The Bells', the Henry Irving part. My dream part! I realised Robert James looked the part more than I did, so I went to his dressing room and said, 'I think you're right for this part, I have to know if you are going to play it. I can't wait!' I was standing

Richard Briers in the 1957 production of 'The Bells', directed by Willard Stoker.

**Opposite** Pauline Yates in 'Dream Girl' by Elmer Rice, 1956.

Harry Baird and Hilary Crane in 'Deep Are The Roots' 1959.

*behind Robert, as he made up for that evening's show. He looked at me in the mirror and I looked at him. He said, 'you really need this part, don't you, well I think you should play it.' I think he possibly had a word with Stoker, it was all sorted. So generous of him, he gave me a wonderful opportunity. Look, that's the photo. It meant that much to me, that I still have it framed."*

Harold Patterson of the U3A in Liverpool recalled his own reaction to *The Bells* – a play that moved him greatly and helped to reinforce his growing love of the theatre. However, it was Richard's incredible and somewhat acrobatic fall backwards at the sounding of the loud and realistic bells, which remains as his abiding image. Apparently, it brought the house down!

Talented local actors were still welcomed into the Company, one such being the tall and handsome Harvey Ashby who had long since atoned for his first stage appearance, aged nine, at Dovedale Road School when he recited a poem backwards! As a high-school boy he was a predecessor of Lennon and McCartney at Liverpool Institute, in the building now occupied by LIPA (Liverpool Institute for the Performing Arts, founded by Paul McCartney). He was a very young member of the Playhouse from 1958 to 1960, a real heartthrob, as remembered by Blue Badge Guide, Valerie Hozack. He came back in 1969 and 1975, his career being mostly in theatre rather than TV or film and he directed as well as performed on stage. Prominent in Equity, the Actor's Union, he was a Council member for many years and Honorary Treasurer in 1992 – 1994. Sadly, his sudden death in 1997, was a cruel blow to his young family, as well as a great loss to Equity.

The 1960 – 1961 season saw Benjamin Whitrow, the previous year's graduate, staying on until the December. During that period he appeared alongside an incredibly youthful-looking John Thaw, the 1960 graduate. For several productions these two young men survived the indignity of a wide range of problems, all synonymous with being the juniors in a company: *A Shred of Evidence* (Whitrow described in review as a miserable blackmailer, Thaw as having patient honesty as the Police Inspector), *All My Sons*, *Thark*, *The Wind and The Rain*, *Candida*, *Juno and The Paycock*, *I Killed the Count* and *Brer Rabbit* (This production is not recalled by Whitrow, but he is listed in the archives as being cast). Benjamin found Willard Stoker a sweet man, but not much help to an insecure beginner:

*"… at the end of a run-through he would clap his hands together and say, 'Well children, wordikins, wordikins,' and that would be your 'note' for the day. I was given my first leading role in 'The Wind and The Rain', an old fashioned piece that had first been done at the Playhouse with Michael Redgrave. Our final Saturday morning run-through was in the week after Remembrance Sunday. Bill [Willard] called me into the stalls afterwards and I thought, 'Hurrah, at last he's going to give me some notes,' he slapped my jacket and said; 'Ben, dear, for God's sake get rid of the dammed poppy!' The Company was excellent, Caro Blakiston, Brenda Kaye, Trevor Baxter, Harvey Ashby. But, I remember the shock when I realised that no one ever talked about the work. It was almost frowned upon. We discussed our next dinner party, or Maud's latest gaffe, but it was a very happy Company. The audience loved to see us exchanging roles every three weeks. Standards, I think, were quite high despite the uninspired choice of repertoire … [my first] season ended with Bill's production of his own musical based on his early life, when a group of travelling players visited his home town [Ormskirk]. It was an intensely sentimental piece called, 'I Remember, I Remember,' [14 June 60] but it was hugely popular. The last night was very emotional as we dismantled the*

*A Paul Mayo design for 'Raquel', Edmund Gray's character from the 1950 production of 'Tobias and the Angel'. [Loaned by the family of Mrs Susan Withers]*

**Opposite** *'The Desk Set' by William Marchand, a comedy about the early days of computers, was the Christmas production in 1957. It was repeated for the BBC in May 1958; several of the cast, including Thelma Barlow, played their original parts but some were unavailable at that time and were replaced by other members of the Rep. company.*

*Opposite John Thaw and Benjamin Whitrow in a 1960 production of 'The Wind and the Rain', directed by Willard Stoker.*

scenery of the play within a play and carried it off stage. Most of the Company were leaving and I experienced my first taste of the real pangs of a Company that had been truly happy together, all splitting up. Oddly I have only worked briefly with anyone from that Company since. I made the mistake of staying on with the 1960 season. John Thaw was the new RADA incumbent. Bill Stoker adored him and he got all the juvenile roles, even Marchbanks in 'Candida'. I received the only entrance round of my life in the first play of the season. The audience always did this when actors from the old Company reappeared in the next season. My last play was, 'I Killed The Count'. I had to say, 'Yes, Sir, I found the Count's gun in the hall table.' I realised this line had hidden dangers and for the most part everything was OK. On the Monday night I said, 'I found the Count's GOWN ...' stopped, giggled and tried to say it again, correctly. This told the audience more clearly than the actual slip. They and all the other actors collapsed and the play came to a halt for two minutes while everyone tried to recover themselves. That was my farewell to Liverpool. It was a happy time."

**Actors associated with the Playhouse who received Knighthoods.** Sir Noel Coward, Sir Michael Redgrave, Sir Rex Harrison, Sir Anthony Hopkins, Sir Ian McKellan, Sir Michael Gambon.

**Winners of RADA Scholarship.** Willard Stoker was the first director at Liverpool Repertory Company to choose a finalist from RADA and offer a one year contract. These scholarships became much sought after and interestingly the records show that all the winners went on to distinguished careers.

| | | | |
|---|---|---|---|
| Margaret Whiting | 1953 – 1954 | performed | 7 roles |
| Terence Knapp | 1954 – 1955 | stayed until 1958 | 48 roles |
| Brian Bedford | 1955 – 1956 | | |
| Richard Briers | 1956 – 1957 | | 16 roles |
| John Stride | 1957 – 1958 | | |
| Caroline Blakiston | 1958 – 1959 | | |
| Benjamin Whitrow | 1959 – 1960 | stayed to end of 1960 | |
| John Thaw | 1960 – 1961 | | 9 roles |

Bedford, Stride, Blakiston and Whitrow – missing programmes do not allow for the accurate recording of the number of roles performed.

## Chapter Four
# A WORLD TO HIDE VIRTUES IN

Bernard Hepton as Thomas More and Peter Needham in Willard Stoker's 1962 production of 'A Man for All Seasons' by Robert Bolt.

The arrival of Bernard Hepton as Artistic Director was significant in that he instituted greater links with the University, brought in the lunch-time readings, and pushed for a better consideration of the needs of actors, especially supporting the argument for time off to fulfil TV commitments. He realised that in order to gain experience, actors needed flexibility in their contracts. His successful approach was to become the pattern for the future. Historically it was a wise move, mirrored by subsequent directors. It was never Hepton's intention to push out the full time resident Company. Hepton is quoted in the Liverpool Daily Post, 3 August 1962 as saying he was, "... firmly of the opinion that the salvation of the theatre was a permanent company". In the present day we see the movement for a return to 'company' structures such as those now being developed at Leeds or at The Orange Tree in Richmond, Surrey. Hepton's rule could be summed up as a greater respect for a balanced use of available acting talent. "Actors are an asset, but in more than an economic sense: they represent a spiritual and artistic value ... they are guardians and executors of texts that, without them, remain only texts." [John Peter. The Sunday Times, 3 January 1999]

1962 goes down in the annals of the Repertory Company as a watershed year. The departure of Maud Carpenter was seen by some as an opportunity, by others as the moment true repertory began to disintegrate. Certainly the plans for the extending of the building put pressure upon everyone involved and an air of, 'Should we extend?' gradually changed to, 'When will we extend?'

Hepton unfortunately left after one year, but not before performing as Thomas More, in A Man for All Seasons by Robert Bolt. It was directed by Willard Stoker, who had returned as Guest Director, even though company members Terence Lodge and Tony Colegate were, by this time, directing plays.

Amidst the turmoil of rebuilding we find Christopher Bullock as Stage Director and later as Theatre Manager. It is greatly to his credit that he devised the new stage and workshop and it was with this advantage that the Company was able to confront the ever-changing face of theatre, now moving into the genre of the spectacular, the big musicals and the challenge of an audience used to 'looking' almost more than they 'listened'.

David Scase was appointed Hepton's successor in 1963 and immediately produced The Rough and Ready Lot by Alun Owen, a local writer. A quirk of fate has however made this production of more lasting interest to Star Trek fans because it represents the first appearance at the Playhouse of Patrick Stewart. Not even the presence of the amiable Philip Hedley, nor the guest appearance of John Slater in A Midsummer Night's Dream can currently compete with the popular interest in Patrick Stewart's being in Liverpool for the 1963 – 1964 season. The TV space traveller appeared in twelve productions and elicited a 'Well done!' from Sidney Jeffery, for his part in The Closing Door. In 1964, his salary was increased by £2 to £23 and he became the top paid actor in the Company at that time. Admittedly less than Cyril Luckham, who appears to have remained the top salaried member of all time within the Company.

The following season, 1964 – 1965, also retains considerable retrospective interest in that in its second production, Sparrers Can't Sing and playing an apparently extremely funny part of a neighbour trying to do a good turn and move an iron bedstead, is a 26-year-old Anthony Hopkins. He disappears for the latter part of November and December but returns in 1965 for the rest of the season. Thus we begin to see the new pattern of flexibility is now well established. For Hopkins, it meant working alongside names which are nowadays as much loved nationally, as his own is internationally – John Savident, Jean Boht, John Hallam, Tony Colegate, Marjorie Yates and others, but not forgetting Lynda Marchal (later Lynda la Plante). She is still remembered for her humour and for

1 2 3
4 5 6 7
8 9

Patrick Stewart montage. Repertory members would usually appear in 8 to 10 productions a year. During his stay in Liverpool, Patrick Stewart, who went on to 'Star Trek' fame was the highest paid member of the cast. A cool £23 a week, a great deal of money in 1964. Other faces in the montage include Jennifer Stirling, Malcolm Reid, Vivien Jones, Cynthia Grenville, Jon Laurimore, Helena de Crespo, Jean Boht, Diana Lyle, and Peter Needham.

working in her dressing room on early writing attempts. Like Beryl Bainbridge before her, she had the opportunity to look and learn, thereby widening her understanding of dramatic structure. Who can say how much unconscious help she received just by being there to absorb the ethos of the building and those who worked in it.

Many of the archive photographs of this time show a young Jean Boht, a native Liverpudlian who has the particular distinction of having an artistic association with Liverpool Playhouse which extends over a thirty year period, and an even longer time as a supporter and regular theatregoer. In 1951 Gerald Cross had rejected her eager application to join the Company. It was not until 1961 that as a 'student' she was allowed to look and learn at one pound a week! She went on to work her way up the ladder of success, via ASM, wardrobe assistant and various bit parts, which added to her modest salary. She described herself as, "… at 26, the oldest Student in the business, but nobody worked harder. I loved every corner of that building. When in the theatre, I was not allowed to address an artiste by their Christian name. I was never allowed to enter the Green Room, except to dress an artiste or make a cup of tea or call them for an entrance". Care of props meant the right to be in the wings during the performance, so Jean had a clear view of a great many of the more experienced cast at work. Jean also found that no matter where she was in the theatre, no matter what she was involved in, she was constantly aware of Maud Carpenter's influence. Willard Stoker was the other influence in her developing theatrical skills and he cast her whenever a suitable part became available.

She describes her first big part as that of a "… middle-aged nasty character who trapped poor old Dulcie Bowman in her house, systematically robbing her of all her furniture and money, whilst pretending to look after her. The Company was rather shocked at Willard letting me do this!" Jean, on the other hand was rather over-worked, not being let off any of her other duties. Life became more relaxed after the departure of Willard and Maud. Jean gradually moved up to the heady heights of full actress, but not before playing a stage management joke on the cast of The Three Cavaliers.

"During the 'snow' scene, we decided to fill the snow shaker with confetti instead of polystyrene chips. Disaster was to strike when a gale blew through the theatre and the poor actors couldn't sing for mouthfuls of the paper and a silent, stern, Christopher Bullock presented me with the Hoover in the interval, and threatened silently – unless the stage was cleared of the stuff before the next act!"

For Jean, the arrival of David Scase as Artistic Director meant promotion, more roles on stage and an up-grade to Stage Manager for other work. Then came responsibility for six new Assistant Stage Managers, all vying for the small bit parts Jean herself had once cherished. After seven quite challenging roles, Jean had had enough, even though she had been working with many wonderful actors. She followed her stars and went on to join the English Shakespeare Company and later returned to the Playhouse to work full time as an actress, rejoining many of her old friends and newcomers, such as Morag Hood. Jean returned again in 1998 in All My Sons. This thirty year gap between appearances at the theatre is exceeded by Gerald Harper's 1952 – 1995, a forty three year difference and by Jean Mills, who as a child in the late 1920s appeared along side Robert Donat and in 1997 in Rebecca the penultimate production of the Liverpool Repertory Company. A gap of seventy years!

With the onset of the regular use of the Studio, or the Theatre Upstairs, as it was originally titled, there was a wider choice of plays for the public and more interesting options for actors and directors. The Osborne play, Look Back in Anger was chosen to open the new performance space on the 29 October 1969. With a growing demand on all the backstage skills, good use was made of the newly built workshop and wardrobe facilities, even though many of the plays were smaller in cast size, or set within a more

## Too few to mention

Ian KcKellen 1969 and Bob Hoskins 1970 are just two of the names who have become labelled at Liverpool as 'Guests'. David Suchet 1972 and 1977, represents a 'guest', but Colin Baker 1972 a 'member.' Other much loved names from this period include Joanna David 1971, William Roache 1971, Ken Dodd 1971 and 1973, David Lloyd Meredith 1972, Elizabeth Bell 1971, John Castle 1971, Gilly Coman 1971 [1980s and 1990s] Nicholas Courtney 1969 [1992], Ronald Cunliffe 1974-75, Vivienne Dixon 1970-75, Kenneth Farrington 1973, [1975, 1976, 1977.] Michael Gambon 1970, Liz Gebhardt 1969 [1974, 1978] Tom Georgeson 1972 [1975, 1987], David Goodland 1973 [1997], Paul Howes 1971 – 1973, Jane Lowe 1971[1973-1980] Frank Middlemass 1971, Robin Nedwell 1972, Alan Partington 1961 – 1962 [1968-70, 1971,1973], Alan Rothwell 1974 - 1979 [1981], Jack Shepherd 1974, Marlene Sidaway 1974 and 1996, Ian Talbot 1969 -1972 [1978 - 1979]

Michael Elwyn and Jane Lowe in the 1976 production of 'Macbeth', directed by Leslie Lawton.

simplified design. A wide range of style and themes was presented each year, for example, amongst others *Prometheus* by Aeschylus, *Heads* by Howard Brenton, *Slag* by David Hare, or *Waiting for Godot* by Samuel Beckett.

There has often been a great deal of friendly rivalry between the companies of the Playhouse and Everyman theatres, but Sam Kelly was brought over in 1973 to play a very good 'Wicked Fairy' for the production of *The Love of Four Colonels*, as remembered by Alan Partington. Alan played the part of the music teacher in *The Prime of Miss Jean Brodie*, directed by Ian McKellen in 1971, which he described as a 'fun' production.

Of the 1975-79 period Walter George, in *A review of the Theatre since 1946*, writes of the effect of the arrival of the new Artistic Director, Leslie Lawton, as creating … "a sense of excitement in and around the theatre before the season started. Feeling that I was imagining this, I asked several colleagues who attended the theatre and they agreed it was so." Lawton opened his season with *Trelawney of the Wells*, it was a success, sufficient to allow Walter George to continue his retrospective comment on Lawton as, "The start of four seasons that could fit in with the Armstrong, Fernald and Stoker years of quality theatre". Again there is a native awareness of something different, which even today is referred to as 'Lawton's Era'.

For some, the highlight was Michael Elwyn's performance in *Macbeth* and for others, Michael Cotterill in *My Fair Lady*. Whatever the choice, Lawton preferred to work with established actors rather than unknowns and hence there was a move away from the calmer, steadier audience response. There is a foreshadowing during this period of the later Kenwright era, where not all big names gave satisfaction.

But the true public perception of this period is that Leslie Lawton was the star on and off the stage and there may well have been some justification for the Robin Thornber review of *Present Laughter* in *The Guardian*, quoted by the admiring Walter George in spite of its implied criticism; "… that at times it may have seemed as if he was turning the theatre into a one man show with a large supporting cast. But it's nearly always been a good show." There can be no doubt of that, but within his approximate four year tenure, Lawton used 325 actors and guests. This was hardly surprising. He frequently had three shows running simultaneously. It is impossible to devote a large section to this period, as few were long term members of the Company. However several short memories from various artistes are recorded in other sections of this book.

Inspiration always follows when an aspiring thespian witnesses a great actor at work. Andrew Schofield remembers seeing Peggy Mount in *The Anniversary* in 1976. Quoted here from a long and detailed taped interview, Andrew recalls;

"She played an obnoxious mother. I really enjoyed the night, but Peggy Mount was fantastic. Jeff Rawle was in it. He was great. He had invited me along, gave us the ticket, because I'd been working with him on a television play which was part of a series called 'Play for Today'. This was one of Willy Russell's first – or second, I can't remember – television plays."

Bill Gaunt, already on site as Associate Director/Actor, took over from Lawton and made a conscious effort to establish a trditional season on a Restoration theme, but after the excitment of Lawson it proved very difficult. Memories of Liz Gebhardt, Sharon Mughan [Maughan], John Woodnutt and others seem to have been overshadowed by the tragic death, from a heart attack, of David Casey, who was appearing as Toad. For years a brass memorial plate to him hung in the foyer of the theatre. It disappeared during a later redecoration and has never been found.

*Some of those who did please the audiences in the 1970s – 1980s included Ken Farrington, Alfred Marks, Janet Suzman, Marius Goring, Alan Rothwell, Linda Polan, David Suchet, Alan Rickman, Ian Ogilvy, Peggy Mount, Frederick Farley, Val Lillee, Paula Wilcox, Barbara Murray, Barbara Flynn, Vanda Godsell, Dilys Watling, and Don Warrington. These are remembered with some affection.*

Programme of 'Blood on the Dole'.

**Opposite** *The 1976 production of the 'The Anniversary', which featured Peggy Mount, Jeff Rawle and Alan Rothwell. It was directed by Malcolm Farquhar.*

During the 1980s, certain actors did appear and re-appear at various times, gaining their place in the memories and affections of various audiences. With the arrival of the youthful and adventurous 'Gang of Four', the programming of new work from a more 'writer led' management began to emerge.

One notable performer at this time was Andrew Schofield, who appeared many times between 1981 and 1997. To continue his taped stories, some are given here, mostly verbatim, but occasionally shortened to accommodate the text:

*"I'm Kirkby born and bred, I still live there … I was playing in a band in a pub in Hardman Street and Willy Russell and Alan Bleasdale came to see us play. I think Jim Morris had just written a play, 'Blood on the Dole' and I was asked to come along and read it. I'd done a television play for Willy, when I was at school, so he still had a memory of me. So then I was more or less given the part … It was in the Studio, there wasn't a big budget, so we were given a ladder, two benches, a wheelbarrow and, if I remember rightly, two scaffolding poles. And out of that it was brilliant of Pip [Broughton] and – who did the design – yes, Ellen Cairns, a lovely Scottish lady who I've worked with many times since. It was a great show and it went down fantastic. A long, deep bow to Jim [Morris], who wrote it, plus the cast was great – John Wild played my mate, Janet Rawson and Gilly Coman were the two girls, and Brian Reagan from 'Brookside'. Later, it went on tour, and Kate Fitzgerald came in to play one of the parts … I'd worked with Kate many years before that, because we'd done this thing in Exchange Flags. It was a piss-take (oh, sorry!) on 'Romeo and Juliet', and that was one of Jim Hitchmough's first things. Jim was a great man and a cracker."*

*'Blood on the Dole' was a great play, Jim (Morris) had a bit of everything in it: it had two lads struggling; one of them ends up going to Ireland; one of them trying to make good for himself instead of being out on the streets, so he does the sewing business. And the girls, he writes some really lovely monologues, the girls talk about the changing face of Liverpool. And then the trauma, the sledgehammer that Jim uses. And it was getting the people into the Playhouse that we wanted to get in, local people, being interested in local writers and local performers.*

*It's funny, it's like I was working a few years later in Spain. And just before the plane took off, this tune came on over the Tannoy, 'Going Home' [he hums the tune] and it was a tune that was used in 'Blood on the Dole'. And I'm sitting there thinking, 'I wonder what John's doing now?' – John Wild, my friend, who was in it. So the plane takes off, thirty thousand feet, who opens the toilet door in the plane? John! John Wild comes out of the toilet door on the same plane. It's true! But he was sitting in another part of the plane, and he'd heard the tune and thought of me. And then he comes out of the toilet door! It was like … smashing!!*

*… 'Not the April the 1st Show', in the Studio, with Chris Bond … we were improvising stuff, writing stuff down, sketches, and writers were coming in, Jimmy McGovern, Jim Morris and Bill Morrison, anyone who wanted to contribute, and we'd sort of work it and have a go at it, and some of the stuff wasn't ready even two weeks into it. It was great, fantastic! The atmosphere in the Studio was always buzzing. I do enjoy the Studio, yes, the thing with the Studio is you can hear people's toenails growing. They are virtually on top of you, so you've got to keep really focused.*

*… The move to the main stage came via Chris Bond, because he did enjoy 'The Not the April the 1st Show', he thought it was great, and he asked if I'd like to write the music for 'Erpingham Camp'. And I said 'What do you mean, write the music? I've never been asked to WRITE it!' But that's typical of Chris Bond, he sort of like throws you in the deep end and says 'Well, you get on with it.' I must say, the music wasn't that good, but it was a great experience playing and working in it. Neil Cunningham*

was great, he was a cracking actor, and who else? – Peter Holmes played the priest in it. Joe Orton – it went down really well, because there was some really funny lines in it. It was great. We played some, like, band that was in the Camp. It wasn't strictly all Joe Orton, because Chris Bond had written things to sort of bring it up a bit, up-to-date as it were, but the laughing was great. I mean, people really accepted it and thought it was fantastic, a good crack, a good night out.

... The thing I really like about Chris Bond is that he's always willing to give you the chance. If he can see something in you, he'll go, 'Yeh, go on!' and you'll say, 'But that's opera singing!' and he'll say, 'So what?' and that's great, it gives you confidence. That's what I love about the man, he's willing to let you have a go.

... Carl Hawkins had actually been there for years. [Laughs] 'The cad!' He had this Stoniers, didn't he? Carl was always a really great bloke, full of enthusiasm, full of tremendous wit, and he was always encouraging. He came to see, up until he became ill, but even then, he came to see everything that was on, and he was always complimentary, as I say, enthusiastic and encouraging, and sadly missed. I always remember him in his Harris tweed and his pipe ... and his 'Jolly good show!'

Willy Russell, Bill Morrison and Alan Bleasdale were always about, too. That period of time does get a lot of knocking, but that's when I joined it, and the thing I liked about it was because it was chaotic ... but I find that out of chaos something's always creating – well, we've got the earth, haven't we? But there was a lot of energy and there was a lot of confusion, but out of that – something good – I think, anyway, something good for me – came out of it, and a lot of people came to see the plays ... I found it a great time. And a lot of the people who were acting, who were on stage – I'm not so sure about the administrative side, that was a different kettle – but I know to actually be working there, to be rehearsing and involved on the stage and performing, it was a great time.

... 'Blood Brothers'? Yes, I was the first narrator. We all met for the read-through in Mathew Street, and I get there and they were all sitting around, and I thought 'Oh, no!' And I go and sit down, and then there's like, 'OK. Let's start. Let's read.' So, we were reading through it and as we were coming to various parts, like Milkman or Judge, Chris Bond would go, 'You can do that, can't you!' 'Oh, er, yeh, OK,' and he'd go, 'yeh, you do that, you play the Bus Conductor.' But I mean, that's what made it work, going from like Mephistopheles-type thing, the devil's advocate type, into the Narrator, into all these other different little parts, that's Chris again, he knows from his experience what works on stage. George Costigan? – he was fun to be with, George, I did get on with him.

And Barbara Dickson; she played the first Mrs Johnson. I've worked with her since. We did 'The Seven Ages of Woman' last year, remember? Barbara did this Mrs Lovett thing, 'Wait, what's your rush, what's your hurry?' from 'Sweeney Todd' [I did that with Chris Bond in 82, wasn't it?]. Anyway, in 'Seven Ages' we did 'When I'm Sixty Four' and Barbara wanted me to resurrect a character I'd done in 'Blood Brothers'. There was that scene when the kids are playing in the street and I'd come out as the old man and go, 'Hey, I'm trying to sleep!' and get my teeth out and go back in. So, she wanted that character to come up out again, and we did, we used to have a laugh.

I've dried twice on stage. I hate talking about it because I sort of get palpitations, as it is, thinking about it! Once was in 'A Man for All Seasons' [at the Anglican Cathedral]. I had to come on and say, 'What is silence?' Thomas More's in court, and he won't denounce something-or-other, and Cromwell says he's more or less guilty by 'silence'. You know what the acoustics are like in the

Andrew Schofield in the 1991 production of 'A Man for All Seasons', at the Anglican Cathedral, directed by Peter Oyston. [photograph Phil Cutts]

**Opposite** 'Down the Dock Road' by Alan Bleasdale, 1976 with Geoffrey Hughes, Christopher Neil, Mickey Finn and Tony Haygarth. Designed by Billy Meall and directed by Brian Howard.

Martin Shaw as Elvis Presley in 'Are You Lonesome Tonight' written by Alan Bleasdale and directed by Robin Lefevre, 1985. [Phil Cutts]

**Opposite** 'The 19th Hole' with Bruce Montague, David Lumsden, Eric Sykes and Alan Bennion, directed by Tony Craven 1992. [Phil Cutts]

Cathedral, echoy, and I'm arguing the case against him, and I say 'What is silence?' Followed by 'silence is … ', and then I dried. Everyone was waiting for the next bit. My shoulders and my neck started tingling and I felt myself imploding and it was all going grey, and I remember sweating, like learning to ride a bike. I don't know how, I just came back with something else, but it was really frightening. The other time was in 'Laughing Wild'. There was a lovely girl called Sheila McNaught. It's a two-hander by Christopher Durang, an American play, put on by the Threadbare Theatre Company, it was directed at that time by Slim Stewart Parry. He and his wife ran that Company. Anyway, there was a line in it about an 'eye'; I can't remember the exact line, but I just dried. And I'll tell you why I dried: I don't normally look around the audience, when I'm doing something, I just don't see them. I don't see anyone, I just sort of keep going. This particular night, my eyes stopped on Ian Kellgren, who looked really bored, and I just went, I dried! I thought he wasn't taking any notice. So then I said – and I've never said anything like it – I said 'Line?', but I said it with an American accent, because I was playing this American, and the prompt, on the book, didn't give it to me. And so I said 'Line!', and she didn't. And so I had to go over to the little gold box, and I said 'LINE!' And the next line was 'Eye … ' and she just thought I was saying 'Eye' four or five times, so it was a big mix-up. But they're the only two times I've really, really gone, like that.

Tom Georgeson? He was there for ages, and I first met him when I was doing 'Scully' for the TV. He was playing a police officer whose face was scarred and one eye was higher than the other, that's why we called him 'Isaiah'. We had a great laugh, Tom and me, and we've been friends ever since. He once wanted me to play 'Hamlet' at the Playhouse, but it just never came about. He's just finished 'L1', you know, the Liverpool thing. He's always working, Tom. He was at the Playhouse for ages. Hero! You must talk to Chris Darwin, another one who's local, and Val Lillee. Don't forget Pauline Daniels and Kate Fitzgerald … I know we were all in love with the place."

Although 'Blood Brothers' is accorded the Victor Ludorum of the 1980s, few who saw the Bill Morrison, Alan Bleasdale production 'Are You Lonesome Tonight' [1985] will forget the magic of Martin Shaw on stage as Elvis. The first of the musical biographies, it perhaps deserved a better shelf life than it achieved. The later production of 'Be-bop-a-lula' with its focus upon Eddie Cochrane and Gene Vincent did achieve tour status and early recognition for the production skills of Ian Kellgren working with Bill Morrison as director of the piece. The musical ability of Andrew Schofield as Gene Vincent was aptly matched by Tim Whitnall as Eddie Cochrane. The presence of Michael Starke, portraying Hal Carter is still a happy memory for 'Brookside' fans.

The late 1980s were to form an interesting 'director-led' programming, much influenced by the associates, Kate Rowland, Peter Oyston, Tal Rubin and later Ramin Grey. Ian Kellgren's personal choices were middle of the road, some would say safe, but he was willing to allow others to diversify to new works. Company wise, the Studio had a group of regulars who, like Andrew Schofield, Noreen Kershaw or Val Lillee, to mention just a few, gave the appearance of a permanency. The main stage, with *Gypsy* as the 1987 Christmas production, had the popular Pauline Daniels as Rose. However, the 1988 production of *Camelot*, the 1989 *Great Expectations* and the 1990 *Around the World in Eighty Days*, each failed to address the need for a local star attraction. And yet each musical demonstrated Kellgren's growing ability to address the demand for spectacular presentation and was increasingly geared to recover the 'subscriber'. The increase of 37% in audience numbers was largely due to the success of computer-aided box office activity, which

could be used to monitor not only the book-keeping, but also the correct audience targeting. Audiences could be more easily categorised by type: schools, family, thirtysomethings, silver, pink, punk or pop! It indicated which members of the audience were selective of shows and those who would loyally support everything. Kellgren, a family-minded man, was acutely aware of the value of balancing the programme to include a fair proportion of work suitable for all age groups, without trying to alienate the intellectual or alternative ideas which percolated through a city with over forty thousand University students. Although prepared to direct work himself, such as *Macbeth*, *Taste of Honey*, *Nuts*, *The Ruling Classes*, *Arsenic and Old Lace* and others, he nevertheless gave the likes of *The Shadow of a Gunman* to Eric Standidge, *Madame Mao*, *Murder in the Cathedral* and *A Man for All Season's* to Peter Oyston, *Crimes of the Heart*, which featured Jacquette May, *North*, *Self Catering* and *Fears and Miseries of the 3rd Reich* to Kate Rowland. This last mentioned production, in the Studio Theatre, was to give a clear indicator of the problems which would come about from the disbanding of the old Merseyside County Council. The Wirral Local Authority threatened to withdraw funding because of the political content of the drama. Kellgren backed Rowland, believing funders must be allowed only a limited say in controlling programming.

The 1990s began with Ian Kellgren's large scale musical presentation of *Great Expectations*, designed by Demetria Hersey and reviewed as, "Demetria Hersey, the designer whose work provides … constant dazzle from the opening at the grim graveside to a nightmare finale. Robert Hands brings human warmth to the role … and Ian Kellgren directs in assured fashion' … 'Ian Kellgren has pulled together a family show which can appeal to all ages and which stints at nothing. Charles Dickens would love it!" [Joe Riley, *Liverpool Echo*] This production amply demonstrated Kellgren's talents and as discussed in Chapter Nine, it retrospectively highlights some of the weaknesses surrounding such an expensive production.

Then there shortly followed *Blues In The Night*, considered one of the best musical presentations ever given at The Playhouse, with Stephanie Lawrence, Miquel Brown, Precious Wilson and Ewen Cummins. Only the 1997 Richard Williams' production of *Mysteries* came near enough to challenge it, in the opinion of enthusiasts of serious harmony.

From 1991, the next five years were characterised by large scale productions touring in or out of the Playhouse under the auspices of the London-based impresario, Bill Kenwright. He writes in the first season brochure that, "… my role as Executive Producer gives me virtual control of the theatre's fortunes – control which excites, frightens and challenges me in the same instant". Ian Kellgren, retained as in-house Artistic Director, was allowed to complete a project which had been dear to his heart, the dramatisation of *An Awfully Big Adventure* by Beryl Bainbridge. Kellgren had always hoped to see the story set upon the stage of the Playhouse and in spite of financial difficulties and delays, this was eventually presented in March 1992, with a cast including Eithne Browne, Richard Stirling, Ian Burford, Rodney Bewes and Tim Woodward. Adapted by her from her original novel, the story line drew heavily on Beryl's images of her own time at the Playhouse. Ian Kellgren, in his foreword to the programme for this production, said, "… It seemed right that it become a play and be performed at the Playhouse". After initial hesitation, Beryl completed the play. The revolve stage used created a grand, if expensive, centre piece to the design.

An unknown, Greg Wise came to Liverpool to portray Jack Good in *Good Rocking Tonite*. Hardly mentioned today, it nevertheless highlighted talented actor/musicians such as Helen Wickens. The following year saw *Imagine* scripted by Jim Hitchmough, Ian Kellgren and Keith Strachan. Twice produced, it is remembered for Mark McGann and Andrew Schofield's equally successful interpretations of John Lennon.

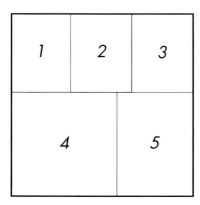

[1] Danny McCall as Billy Fury in 'The Sound of Fury', 1995. [2] Gerry Marsden as himself and Carl Kirshner as the young Marsden in 'Ferry Cross the Mersey', 1996. [3] Andrew Schofield as John Lennon in 'Imagine', 1994. [4] Mark McGann as John Lennon in the 1992 production of 'Imagine'. [5] Karl Lornie as Paul McCartney in 'Sgt Pepper's Magical Mystery Trip', 1997. [all photographs Phil Cutts]

Maggie Norris and Guy Picot's *Ferry Cross the Mersey* was to get high box office returns, but then it did have the advantage of a longer run and prices were slightly higher. The presence of Gerry Marsden himself was also a considerable pull, as was Danny McCall in *The Sound of Fury* which had followed a similar pattern of production.

*Robin, Prince of Sherwood* by Rick Fenn and Peter Howarth had a very different presentation and toured for Bill Kenwright Limited for several years. Popular with the Playhouse's more traditional audience, it did not appeal to the 'bopping and popping' section of the community. Jon Miller and Shirlie Roden's musical biography of Roy Orbison, *Only The Lonely,* also began life at the Playhouse and toured for several years, whereas Shirlie Roden's *Sleeping Beauty* was intended as a special for the young. Because of Bill Kenwright's insistence upon the music being maintained at 'pop' levels, the Director, Henry Metcalfe, had to go out front before each performance and talk to the matinee audience. His method of selecting a child to decide how loud the drums should 'roll' worked well and the initial reactions from the early performances, when many mothers left with crying children, gradually ceased. Kenwright also brought in Willy Russell's *Blood Brothers* with Stephanie Lawrence in the lead and Warwick Evans as narrator.

Audience numbers at all Bill's musicals were good, especially for the initial production runs. However, the poor attendance figures for some of the repeated shows, such as *Robin, Prince of Sherwood* or *Only the Lonely*, must have been a disappointment to him. Gradually the predominance of 'rock' drove away the long term subscriber more interested in a Repertory style of performance, the more serious theatregoer who remembered St John Ervine's injunction, 'Don't come to the theatre and leave your brains in the cloakroom!'

Nevertheless, the popular *No Trams to Lime Street*, whilst it had a poignancy because of the death of Alun Owen the writer, is remembered by Liverpudlians because it returned Tony Scoggins to the stage. Tony joined the Board of the Theatre as a Local Councillor for Knowsley, giving valuable service as a knowledgeable link between the concerns of Local Councils and the needs of a theatre. He was later joined on the Board by Dean Sullivan of *Brookside*. Both these men fully endorsed the successful repertory methods re-introduced by Richard Williams.

**The last scene of all.** There had been no true resident repertory company since the 1979 – 1981 company, under Bill Gaunt. Indeed few at the theatre had any experience of a 'Rep' company of actors. Therefore, in the August of 1996, the idea of a resident Repertory Company of performers was greeted by many of the Playhouse staff with restrained enthusiasm. Delighted to have the management of production as completely in-house once more, nevertheless, for most of the younger members, the idea of a resident Company of players was a new, and to them, an untried method of production. Where were the stars to sell the shows? How could the same actor fit into such a demanding cycle of work? For others, like the designer and scenic painter Billy Meall, with memories of working at the Playhouse in the 1960s, it was a moment of supreme excitement. Billy Meall's approbation was crucial to the growing support for Richard Williams, which gradually came about from the grassroots of the in-house staff. Similarly, the support of Keith Wolfenden as Company Stage Manager gave Williams himself the opportunity to take things at a steady and unassertive pace. Gradually with the backing of these two mature and able men, a stability returned to the Playhouse, which was consolidated by the arrival of Jane Dawson, in April 1997, as Administrative Director and Tim Higham as Production Manager.

Williams' programme opened on the 11 September 1996 with *Noises Off* by Michael Frayn. The shock for many of the audience

Paul Ryan.

**Opposite** 'Noises Off', 1996, Richard Williams'
production of the new season's company shows
Paul Ryan, Marlene Sidaway, Elizabeth Elvin and
Victoria Gay. [Phil Cutts]

was in the loss of Kenwright glamour, both in terms of names and set design. It was obvious that here was a company prepared to 'cut its cloth' in cost but without harming the 'width' of performance. For the first time Liverpool met Paul Ryan, Felicity Duncan, Victoria Gay, Joseph Noble, Paul Gilmore, Godfrey Jackman and Elisabeth Elvin, knowing that they would be seeing them in the follow-on productions. He gave the worried publicity department a 'guest appearance' of Marlene Sidaway to give their efforts a 'name' from a recent TV serialisation of *Pride and Prejudice*. Eight months later he gave them Elizabeth Kelly, [Auntie Nellie in *Eastenders*] and in the following November, in the Company's penultimate production, a return visit by Peter Birch, at that time a TV *Casualty* personality. Williams took things carefully and booked actors on the principle of cost effectiveness as well as ability. The likes of Joseph Noble who could sing, dance and act, made him a valuable Company member, but it was the almost mesmerising versatility of the energetic Paul Ryan which eventually won the audience round to the idea of having their 'own' company once again. Ryan's energy was infectious, younger performers such as Iain Jones and Damian Gaskin, were helped by working alongside him, and he was almost overwhelmingly at his best when cast in quick change character roles within a play. Few who saw his move from Lysander to Quince have forgotten his genius. His angel to devil in *The Mysteries* or his multiple *Bouncers* characters, some so evil, some so wittingly feminine, that you forgot this was one man playing all roles. Paul Ryan, himself, gives this grateful memory of his time at Liverpool.

> "My time at the Playhouse represents the most enjoyable, varied and productive period of my career thus far. With Richard Williams as Artistic Director, any actor who appeared on the stage in the theatre's last sixteen months was guaranteed at least two things: a great laugh (rehearsals were always a jolly affair), and the opportunity to take risks in the choices one made regarding characterisation. Oh yes, there was a third thing that was always part of the package; you would be working with good actors in an atmosphere that was always positive and supportive. Richard ran the place like a true rep of the old style – he had a pool of actors who would appear and re-appear, giving the audience the chance to get to know the actor and in turn giving the actor the chance to play a whole variety of roles. I, myself, appeared in nine productions including Shakespeare, high comedy, epic theatre, gothic drama and a couple of Christmas shows. I sang ditties, arias, Gospel hymns and opera. I was a scarecrow, a rat, a night-club bouncer, a lover, a fighter, a female, a cocaine-riddled accountant, a lawyer, a cad and a sex-starved estate agent. It's a heck of a list and I'll admit to being proud of it, but these sort of experiences are becoming more and more rare for actors these days. With the closure of the Company goes yet another opportunity for actors, young and old, to go through the learning experience that is so often rep theatre. But, with luck, the Playhouse itself is not to shut forever, and with a little more luck a few of us will be there on the opening night. See you then!" [Paul Ryan, Company Member, August 1996 – January 1998]

During Ryan's eighteen months with the Company and working alongside Company members on shorter term contracts, such as Keiron Smith, Adam Stafford, Martin Scott Gilmore, Melissa Collier, David Goodland, Cheryl Fergison, Jo Castleton, Charles Millham, or Paul Basson, the benefits of such a talent as Paul Ryan's to the development of customer loyalty became obvious. The audience began again to appreciate the actor's skill, rather than the hyped stage or TV personality. Profits began to be seen in terms other than just money. It was the gradual return of the Playhouse to ordinary people who wanted a night out at a theatre which had become familiar, not only because of its building, but more importantly because of a growing bond between the actors and the people of Merseyside. Here, at last, was a return to the commitment of the principles of repertory.

Within every seasonal cycle of plays there was something for everyone. Gradually both the 'Rock and Rollers' and the moneyed classes lost their stranglehold on the Playhouse. The ordinary, non-regular theatre-going public was given four weeks of Margi Clarke in *Nightcollar* by the local writers, Powell and Furlong. The culture vultures had a week of the RSC. Young children were given the classics, *Wind in the Willows* and *The Wizard of Oz*, with more matinee performances and no heavy rock and roll music, which particularly delighted parents and primary schools teachers. Teenagers complained about the loss of this type of music, but on the whole it was welcomed. The building is too small for such intrusive and all pervasive music. The gentler use of the piano, and no more than three-piece ensembles, gradually became a welcome addition to productions requiring live musical support. In this matter the Repertory Company was helped by Richard Williams' wife, the pianist Joanna MacGregor. Joanna became a familiar figure at the theatre. Her work seldom adequately compensated, she nevertheless joined a growing band of professionals who came forward to 'volunteer' or to work for reduced fees, in order to see the dream become a reality; the likes of the designer, David Collis, or the scenic painters, Chris Rehill and Geoff Cook and many other volunteers, too numerous to list here, but whose contributions were invaluable.

Eighteen months after he took up the position of Artistic Director, Richard Williams faced the final production with a heavy heart. [The issues concerning the Board and the 1995 Inland Revenue debt are dealt with in Chapter Nine, The Achilles Heel] Without the support of Jane Dawson, the entire period leading up to the closure of the Company would have been considerably more difficult, not only for Williams, but for all staff members.

Made redundant during the 1991 crisis while working for Elizabeth Ann Meacham, in the publicity department, Martin Scott Gilmore went on to realise his dream of getting into drama college. Once qualified, his ambition was to appear with the Liverpool Rep. He managed to be available to play the Tin Man in *The Wizard of Oz* and says of that time, "Playing the Tin Man was a challenge to create 'metallic' movement, sound and gesture. I produced his clanking sound by putting nuts and bolts in a sweet tin attached to my silver boots." Considering the sadness back stage as the countdown to closure approached, Martin wrote, "There was virtually no money for *The Wizard of Oz*. The production had a strong design, but was stripped down to the barest minimum. It was raw talent, charisma and sheer determination from the actors and crew that made the final show the great success it was. It was an exhilarating, yet also depressing show to work on. We were a happy and strong Company, winning the audiences, but backstage there was a tense and frustrated atmosphere, as each day another long-standing employee was made redundant." The irony of the situation was not lost on Martin. Six years on from his own redundancy, it was his turn to console his former head of department, Elizabeth Ann Meacham, as she received her notice.

*Martin Scott Gilmore.*

**Opposite** *'The Wind in the Willows' by Kenneth Grahame was first dramatised by AA Milne, as 'Toad of Toad Hall'. Liverpool Playhouse gave the world premiere in 1929. The first 'Toad' was Leslie Kyle [opposite right] and the last of the six Playhouse 'Toads' was Charles Millham [opposite left], in Andy Rashleigh's version in 1996. [Christine Mathews-Sheen]*

### The final list of redundancies included amongst others

Caroline Parry, Tim Higham, Frances Stokes, Pat Breen O'Neill, Alan McCracken, Susan Thompson, Susanna Turner Wilson, Chris Duffy, Eloise Attwood, Melanie Dodd, Elizabeth Ann Meacham, Karen Syme, Kenny Hammond, Slim Stewart-Parry, Catrin Williams, Kelly Smith, Alice Bennett, Carol Walker, Gloria Ashworth, David Murray, Kate Stewart, Steve Threlfall, Morag Murchison, Gary Sanderson, Rob Beamer, George Smith, Anne-Marie Allison, Heather Brocklesby, Denise Walker, Gary Hesketh, Richard Baxter, Alan Howe, Billy Meall, Lisa Walker, Beryl Smith, Chris Trigg, Kevin Tiernan, Margaret Halpin, all bar and restaurant staff, cleaners and part-time and volunteer ushers and part-time box office staff.

*Tony Scoggins, Dean Sullivan and Mickey Starke of Mersey TV's Brookside.*

**Opposite** *Slim Stewart Parry and Kenny Hammond on the 3rd January 1998. [Anne Gilmore]*

**Farewell to Repertory, 3 January 1998.** A packed house, the Company and audience singing *Somewhere Over the Rainbow*, and the tears and fears of the departing crowds will remain with all who attended that last night of the Liverpool Repertory Company. Hollow promises were sent through the crowds and, like a game of Chinese whispers, nobody knew for certain who was speaking the truth. Many sensed that official Arts Council and Local Authority murmuring of, 'the phoenix rising from the ashes', were to prove far from the truth. They clung to the one certainty that, as a listed building it had to reopen as a theatre. But, they also knew that their theatre needed the life blood of a company to give it that 'je ne sais quoi' that made the old building breathe with a vitality which "… moved plays to the people and people into plays …" On that night all understood Harold Brighouse's words.

That night was also particularly poignant for the two men who had been responsible for security and fire safety at the theatre for many years. Slim Stewart Parry was a Company man in the very best sense of the word. He had worked as an associate director, as a writer, as a festival organiser, had overseen several new writing projects, as well as run his own production company. Like Robert James and so many others before him, he was always prepared to undertake any task to maintain the work of the theatre. Thus it was that on the last night he was fire officer, alongside the equally loyal and energetic, Kenny Hammond.

Kenny Hammond, as the Theatre's Security guard, was to be the last to hand over his keys and leave on the night of 3 January 1998. Sadly, Kenny died later that same year and never returned to his beloved theatre. It was a mark of the 'Family' which had re-formed during the post-Kenwright years, that seventeen members of the staff, including Richard Williams himself, attended Kenny's funeral. His death saddened many of the public, especially disabled theatregoers, such as Mrs Vera Dev and Mrs Sue Byrne, who had valued his help whenever they attended the theatre.

The last paid employee of the Liverpool Repertory Company was Sue Thompson, who was responsible for tidying up the remnants of the Company's book-keeping.

## Chapter Five
## LOOK AT ME I'M ACTING

The Herculean task of acting may terrify the beginner, may well exhaust the seasoned veteran, and can definitely humiliate the over-confident. It can annihilate the dross of the profession in the space of any one performance. Producers and directors alike may claim that funding is their biggest headache, but without the malleable talent of the true performer, all monies would be wasted. Large-scale productions may sometimes mask the weakness of an individual actor; equally the dominance of another could destroy the balance within a play. The most successful actor is the one who can take direction, sustain the part within the balance of the whole, and not seek to impose the actor's own personality upon the character. The best in the profession make continual use of good voice and dialect coaches. Actors enjoy working with those directors whose energy and insight into the intentions of the writer enable them to develop and utilise their acting skills.

Sometimes things go wrong. From the programme for the 29 November 1948, comes the following: "Life here in the weeks running up to the festive season is a nightmare of fun. It started three weeks ago. *The Provoked Wife* running in the evenings, rehearsal for *When We Are Married* during the day, freely interspersed with music rehearsals for *The Silver Curlew*. The beauty and simplicity of life can be fully appreciated when doing three things at once – and wondering what to get Aunt Martha for Christmas. The fact the Sir John Vanburgh's script is in 18th Century English, *When We Are Married* in Yorkshire, and *The Silver Curlew* in Norfolk dialect, is a mere bagatelle. Of course they all come through to you [the audience] just the same because we've all got colds."

The knock-on effect of witnessing a performer in many different roles is that young people can learn what acting is all about. Local lad Derek Nimmo is one who openly acknowledged his youthful admiration for Cyril Luckham, and his delight when, in the 1970s, they were performing together in the *Oh, Brother* and *Oh, Father* television series. Nimmo says, in the *Liverpool Daily Post* in 1973, "I used to often wait outside the stage door but never dared to stop him to talk. He was my idol and it took twenty-five years to join him in *Oh, Brother*."

The Rep has always had an interest in local beginners, especially the young. The last two productions of the Liverpool Repertory Company are clear indicators of this trend. In *Rebecca*, the professional debut of Melanie Gutteridge, playing Mrs de Winters, was effectively low key in comparison to the excitement of the last production, *The Wizard of Oz*, which re-introduced 15-year-old Elizabeth Lovelady, with four previous Playhouse productions to her credit and also became the vehicle for the Playhouse debut of 11-year-old Melissa Clarke. Perhaps the fact that Melissa was believed to be the youngest ever Dorothy, in a professional production of the show, may have added to the ripples of press attention afforded these two talented members of local drama schools.

John Arnatt recalls the marathon performances of Abraham Sofaer as King Lear. In 1947, there was some sort of national power problem which meant that matinees had to be played at 5.30 instead of 2.30. "I remember Abraham Sofaer claiming that he must be the only actor to have played *Lear* uncut, twice nightly. He had the most magnificent voice I have ever known and he could, and did, do it."

Ted Valentine gave the fullest version of one of the favourite Maudisms concerned with the art of acting.

"One Thursday afternoon in 1948, John Gielgud's production of 'The Lady's Not for Burning' was playing at the Royal Court and several of the cast came to see a matinee performance of a François Mauriac play at the Playhouse. During an interval, someone told Maud that the tall, slim gentleman with the bald head, sipping his coffee, was John Gielgud. She felt that she should make a distinguished actor feel welcome and went to have a word with him. She introduced herself and Gielgud said

*'Rebecca', with Peter Birch and Melanie Gutteridge in the 1997 production directed by Richard Williams. This was Melanie's debut performance as a professional actress. [Phil Cutts]*

*'I saw in 'The Stage' the other week that John Fernald is to leave his post as Director here, later this year, to take up working at RADA and that your new Director is to be someone called Gerald Cross. Is that the same Gerald Cross who is giving such a fine performance in this afternoon's play?' 'Yes,' said Maud, 'but he won't be acting when he's directing. I mean, you can't do both in the same play, can you?' Gielgud choked slightly on his Rich Tea biscuit. He said 'Well, madam, some of us try'. One remembered newcomer, fresh out of University, was Trevor Danby, who was brought in, as many youngsters were, to help with props, stage managing and to learn the craft by watching their elders and betters. Willard Stoker gave him various walk-on parts as a sugaring to keep the lad eager. A self-confession is the kindest way of revealing the lad's overdoing of a simple task.*

*All I had to do was enter and cross the room of a gentlemen's club and offer a letter on a tray to one of the leading characters with some excruciatingly obvious remark like, 'A letter has arrived for you, sir'. I decided the only way to get noticed was to prolong the action for as long as possible. The first night saw a respectably old man offering slow, constrained but efficient service, but by the end of the first week the character already looked indecently old to be in any kind of active employment – you could almost feel the audience placing mental bets on whether this aged figure would, in fact, ever reach the other side of the room. Finally, the leading man decided 'enough was enough' and having taken the letter, he hastened me off with a gentle push. I was totally in the part, and wholly in keeping with the character's proximity to death, tottered sideways, ever on the brink of total collapse, the entire width of the stage and out of the door in one continuous movement. It brought the house down, and probably quite wrongly, it must be said, got the biggest mis-placed laugh of the night. I was put on the carpet after that and told to be professional in a way that contributed to the play as a whole, but there was thereafter always a feeling of illicit triumph in having completely lost myself in a part. If I can do that, I must be an actor, I thought!"*

When Bernard Hepton directed *King Lear* at the Playhouse in 1963, he engaged the Merseyside pop music group, The Scaffold (famous for their recordings of *Thank U very much* and *Lily The Pink*) to appear as attendants to the Dukes of Cornwall and Albany. At a fairly late stage of rehearsal, he instructed them that, in the first scene when Lear gives each of his elder daughters a large share of his kingdom, the group should register their pleasure and delight. On the first night, he was surprised to see them strutting around the stage, hands clasped above their heads like boxers and acknowledging the roars of laughter and delight from the audience. They felt the volume of approval they had won from the audience at this point was so overwhelming, that they refused Bernard Hepton's pleas to them to cut the 'business'.

Less energetic, was the acting debut of Rupert Bates, the son of Alan. Working as an ASM, he eagerly awaited the opportunity to act. Eventually it came, his big part, which he rehearsed assiduously – a dead body! Opportunity to experiment as an actor often requires a courageous director. As Gilbert Wynne recalls:

*"Dick Tuckey used to work well into the evening, long after we'd stopped rehearsing, with Ken Dodd who was to play Malvolio in 'Twelfth Night'. Dodd gave a wonderful performance as Malvolio; the curtain calls were great. He always gave the audience ten minutes of the funniest jokes I've ever heard and each night different jokes. After the play one night, he presented my mother and aunts with a tickling stick each – you can imagine the comments. One night he gave a marvellous Scouse party, with lots of beef stew and drinks."*

Ken Dodd as Malvolio in Dick Tuckey's 1971
production of 'Twelth Night'.

**Opposite** Gerald Cross in 'Richard II' directed by
Michael Mac Owen, 1951. [Chambre Hardman]

'King Lear', February 1947, still with post
War austerity in force. Abraham Sofaer
and John Arnatt on stage with direction
believed to be by John Fernald. Most of
this production was affected by a series of
national power failures which caused the
timing of performances to be changed,
often at short notice.

Ian McKellen appeared and directed at the Playhouse. Pictured here in the 1969 production of 'The Bacchae', directed by Dick Tuckey.

**Opposite** 'The Prime of Miss Jean Brodie', 1969 including, amongst others Jane Nicholson, Cheryl Murray, Marcelle Livingstone, Jackie Fishel, Jane Brown, Liz Gebhadt, Geraldine Ewing and Gilly Coman, directed by Ian McKellen.

**Knowing your words.** Frederick Farley is remembered, by Ted Valentine, for helping an actor who 'dried' on stage:

*"During a performance of Edward Wooll's courtroom drama 'Libel', Freddy, as counsel for the prosecution, was cross-examining a witness, when the witness dried stone dead. Freddy knew the cross-examination needed to be played at top speed and since it was clear that no reply was immediately forthcoming, he said 'Let me rephrase that', and repeated the cue in slightly different words. Still no response. After another couple of attempts by Freddy to give the other actor time to remember, equally futile, he stopped and, in the pause, the prompt came. After the scene, I'm fairly sure it was Caroline Blakiston who said 'You see – if you dry, just keep cool – there is no substitute for Wooll!'" (Reference to a popular advertisement of the time. Some backstage teasing can be more ferocious.)*

On a more serious note, secure knowledge of the script does not necessarily result in a satisfying performance. Ronald Herdman would go over his lines before each performance, for the previews and first night of *Mrs Warren's Profession* in 1968, but felt as though he was on automatic pilot. The next night, he wiped the lines from his mind until the curtain went up. He was terrified, but found that he could then romp through the scenes as freshly as though it was the first time, a valuable lesson for his future career.

**The Snow Queen**. On 23 December 1969: During the time of Anthony Tuckey, Sharon Mughan was at the very beginning of her career and is remembered by Miss Marjorie Tickle for 'corpsing' during a matinee when she had to be disguised as a tree. All the children became very excited and started shouting, "He's behind you!" etc, except one little boy who shouted louder than the rest: "Be careful! It's only a tree dressed as a tree." Everybody, even the actors, laughed. Sally Gibson, in the part of the Snow Queen, bemused many youngsters by appearing to shrink when she was seen off stage. The truth was she performed the queen's part sitting on Sid Livingstone's shoulders, a difficult balancing act, especially as he had to dance with her perched there. To make that possible, Cathy Alger, the wardrobe mistress, made him a crinoline with a decorative panel of vision net down the front, so that he could see where he was going.

**The tummy rumble or the burp!** From a programme cameo on Cynthia Grenville in 1964: "A personal memory of her role of Meg in *The Hostage*, she was required to drink several bottles of stout during the course of the play. By 10pm on dress rehearsal day, the strain of the previous twelve hours began to tell on the cast. During a quiet scene, Cynthia suddenly made the kind of involuntary noise that indicated that the large quantity of stout was at war with her digestive system. She peered into the auditorium and said, 'Blimey, I bet that's not in the script!' Everyone roared with laughter and the ease and flow so necessary in a Behan play was recaptured at once. A timely piece of improvisation, by a mistress of it."

**Gilly Coman.** Many a Liverpool youngster dreams of a stage career. They seldom give up hope and are continually inspired by stories of others whose roots were similar to theirs and who have found a successful career, such as Gilly Coman, a Liverpool girl who had stars in her eyes from the age of three.

Her enthusiasm was nurtured by seeing the Christmas shows at the Playhouse and at other Liverpool theatres. She remembers the excitement, the colours and the music. Her parents owned the GHC Dancing Academy for ballroom dancing (off Smithdown Road,

Sefton Park). Originally this building was a bakery. Later in life Gilly moved to a house in a road called Boswell Street in Toxteth. Gilly was Aveline in the TV series *Bread*, with the family name of Boswell and she looks back with amusement at the strange coincidences typical of her road to success. Hard work also played a part. She began her training as a small girl with the Shelagh Elliott Clarke School of Dance and Drama, which she attended until she was sixteen. Gilly tells us the story of an even stranger coincidence, the stuff dreams are definitely made of – her debut on TV. This resulted from a chance meeting with a director who, after days of unsuccessful auditioning in Leeds, London and Liverpool of hundreds of eager youngsters, caught sight of a vivacious and excited twelve-year-old Gilly meeting Margot Fonteyn. Her excitement was natural, she had just been to the Royal Court to see Margot in *Swan Lake* and, to finish her birthday treat had tea at the Adelphi Hotel, when all the fates brought Margot, arms full of flowers, through the swing doors and face to face with a twelve-year-old asking for her autograph. The weary casting director, about to leave the hotel, stopped in his tracks and stared in wonder. Gilly's mother, Jessie Coman, was worried by this man who proceeded to circle Margot and Gilly, his face one of complete amazement. She admits her first reaction was horror and suspicion. She took a lot of convincing but eventually she accepted his business card. From this stranger than fiction incident, Gilly went on to star in a 'Drinka pinta milka day' ad, and soon into other TV work.

As a pupil of the Elliott Clarke School she was sent for audition at the Playhouse in 1969 for *The Prime of Miss Jean Brodie*. Along with Liz Gebhardt (later in *Please Sir* with John Alderton) and Cheryl Murray (later known as Elsie Tanner's lodger in *Coronation Street*), Gilly found herself in the front of the classroom. She recalls one memorable corpsing incident: as Geraldine Ewing (Miss Brodie) announced the death of one of the characters in the play, they all started to laugh. "Fine for the others, they were facing up stage, but for me, no! I was facing down stage in full view of the audience. I had to disguise my uncontrollable fit of laughter into 'tears of remorse' and exit as fast as I could through the classroom door. Once off stage, I hid in the loo. It is a moment I'll never forget and a show I'll always treasure."

Some time later, during several other appearances at the Playhouse, including *Blood on the Dole* and *Ladies in Waiting*, Gilly's designer husband, Phil Cutts, at that time part of the theatre's design team, began taking photographs of Gilly in rehearsal. These were so popular with everyone who saw them, that he was invited to be the official photographer of the Playhouse. Eventually he took on many other north-west theatres. His distinctive style and thorough work is much appreciated and many examples are to be found in this book.

On one occasion, Gilly found herself drawn into a situation which she recalls as one of the challenges of her career. Alan Bleasdale rang her on a Friday night with a cry for help. *Having a Ball* was about to open when the leading lady fell ill with septicaemia. Alan's plea was answered with a "Yes", followed by a weekend of concentrated study to learn lines, "made easier by the brilliant dialogue", and with little rehearsal, the support given by a grateful cast, all helping her achieve in three days, what normally would require three weeks rehearsal.

Another pupil of Shelagh Elliott Clarke's School, whose first stage appearance was at the Playhouse, was Steven Mathers. Later, his first job after drama school was also at the Playhouse, in Willy Russell's *Stags and Hens* in 1982 – he says of that devasting experience – "No lines, but I had to vomit on cue several times each night."

One of the questions asked of everyone interviewed was, "Can you remember your first ever visit to a theatre?" Many recalled it

*William Gaunt and Gilly Coman in Alan Bleasdale's 'Having a Ball', directed by Pip Broughton, 1990. [Phil Cutts]*

as being to the Playhouse. One who didn't was Andrew Schofield, quoted from a long taped interview:

*"... it was when I went to the theatre with my dad – he was a welder and he used to work for a company called Tubewrights, and they used to give you a Christmas 'do' and we'd all jump on a chara and go down – and we went to the Royal Court and saw Ken Dodd and his Diddymen. I loved it as a kid. I must have been about – I don't know – six, seven. But the first time I went sort of like a teenager, it was to go and see a brilliant play. It was at the Everyman, and it was called 'Funny Peculiar.' There was Pete Postlethwaite, Julie Walters and a fantastic performance, which I thought was brilliant, and I've told him since: playing the village idiot, for want of a better word, was Matthew Kelly. He was fantastic, and it was a great cast – I remember it all."*

**The Henry Cotton Memorial Fund.** The plight of struggling arts students is well documented and was one which keenly interested Henry Cotton, a much respected and well liked local business man, as well as President and past Chairman of the Company. Following his untimely death, an appeal was launched which led to the setting up of the annual prize for students in the Arts. It is run as a charity and is administered by a team from all areas of the arts in Liverpool. At a Gala Night to launch the appeal, the significance of the return of two former Liverpool employees who came to take part in the evening, cannot be overlooked.

Martin Scott Gilmore had, as an almost penniless student with no hope of any grant to see him through his training, been the first ex-Playhouse staff member to instigate a system of patronage by ordinary people to help him with his own funding. Many drama students in recent years have had to find in the region of forty thousand pounds to cover three years tuition and living expenses. Martin was much publicised and, as a result, Damian Gaskin and Kenneth Lanceley, both former employees of the Company, went on to use variations of the system. Many local people on Merseyside thus became patrons of the Arts in a new and accessible way. Their greatest pleasure, the updating of news of their protégés. Eventually, knowing Henry Cotton's interest in Arts training, the need for the Henry Cotton Memorial Fund was more clearly recognised by everyone. Indirectly helped by the publicity given to these young students. The Fund was initiated at a special gala event to which Damian Gaskin had brought several first year students from Bristol to perform short sketches from *She Stoops to Conquer*, the first time he had performed on a professional stage. "A year later, when reserves were running low, I was nominated. I was greatly honoured to find I had been chosen and not only received a beautiful certificate from William Gaunt, but also a financial element that helped me finish my second year of studies." Later Damian was generously helped by Sir Anthony Hopkins, as well as by his many local patrons who sponsored him at twenty pounds a year for three years. His energy in running marathons, putting on plays, selling at car boot sales and a hundred other activities was an impressive record of personal achievement. Many stars of stage and screen were equally impressed by this young man and came to his aid, but he unashamedly admits it was the Friends of Liverpool Playhouse who were his favourite patrons. Their hampers of food and toiletries kept him as the best fed and cleanest student. And he jokingly pointed out that he had the cleanest teeth, thanks to Martin's Scott Gilmore's own Mum – she kept him in toothpaste for three years!

Each in his own way has striven to repay the local community which sponsored them. Damian ran the Starmakers, a serious training programme for young would-be actors, for two years. Martin visited hospitals to entertain, particularly Alder Hey Children's Hospital during the run of *The Wizard of Oz*.

*Some locals who found opportunity via the Playhouse*

Jean Alexander, Beryl Bainbridge, Tom Baker, Steven Berkoff, Joy Blakeman, Jean Boht, Tony Booth, Eithne Browne, Gilly Coman, Trevor Danby, Pauline Daniels, Ken Dodd, Ebony, Kate Fitzgerald, Damian Gaskin, Martin Scott Gilmore, John Gregson, Deryck Guyler, Rex Harrison, Philip Hedley, Bill Kenwright, Noreen Kershaw, Ken Lanceley, Val Lillee, the McGann brothers, Roger McGough, Norman Rossington, Patricia Routledge, Andrew Sachs, Andrew Schofield, Tony Scoggings, Gerald Sim, Ann Stallybrass, Michael Starke, Rita Tushingham, Colin Welland, Michael Williams.

Some of the Munchkins from the 1997 production 'The Wizard of Oz'. [Ann Gilmore]

**Opposite** Damian Gaskin. [Phil Cutts]

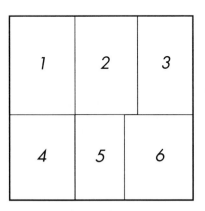

*Notable guests of stage and screen, [1] Daniel J Travanti. [2] Stefan Denis. [Phil Cutts] [3] Roy Marsden. [4] Richard Todd. [5] George Chakiris. [Phil Cutts] [6] Frank Middlemass.*

**The untrained and the unnamed.** Sometimes the situation is saved by the total amateur, as happened during the 1952 season of A *Midsummer Night's Dream*. The actor playing Egeus failed to appear for a matinee and there was no understudy since all the stage management team were already playing small parts. However, a group of Liverpool University students were 'walking on' as Theseus' attendants. One of them had had some experience as an actor and was invited to read the part of Egeus. Ted Valentine was standing in the prompt corner when Maud appeared behind him and whispered, "What's he doing? He's got a book in his hand!" Ted explained the situation and Maud replied, "Oh, I see, but it looks so bad, reading a book. Can't he make it up?"

For the non-theatregoer! Soap stars and series actors who went on to, or came from, famous soaps or filmed series.

| | | | | | |
|---|---|---|---|---|---|
| Jean Alexander | *Coronation Street* | Stella Gonet | *House of Elliott* | Christopher Ravenscroft | *Ruth Rendell Mysteries* |
| | *Last of the Summer Wine* | Deryck Guyler | *Sykes* | David Rintoul | *Dr Finlay's Case Book* |
| Tony Anholt | *Howard's Way* | Robert Hands | *House of Elliott* | William Roache | *Coronation Street* |
| Colin Baker | *Dr Who* | Patricia Hayes | *Till Death Do Us Part* | Patricia Routledge | *Keeping Up Appearances* |
| Jean Boht | *Bread* | Geoffrey Hughes | *Coronation Street* | Andrew Sachs | *Fawlty Towers* |
| Tom Baker | *Dr Who* | | *Keeping Up Appearances* | John Savident | *Coronation Street* |
| Roy Barraclough | *Coronation Street* | Celia Imrie | *Dinner Ladies* | Andrew Schofield | *GBH, Scully* |
| Thelma Barlow | *Coronation Street* | Geraldine James | *Band of Gold* | Paul Shane | *Hi De Hi!, You Rang, M'Lord* |
| Alfie Bass | *Bootsie and Snudge* | Elizabeth Kelly | *EastEnders* | Marlene Sidaway | *Pride and Prejudice* |
| Rodney Bewes | *The Likely Lads* | William Kenwright | *Coronation Street* | Patrick Stewart | *Star Trek* |
| Richard Briers | *The Good Life* | Dervla Kirwan | *Ballykissangel* | Michael Starke | *Brookside* |
| Paul Broughton | *Brookside* | William Lucas | *Black Beauty* | Anne Stallybrass | *The Onedin Line* |
| Eithne Browne | *Brookside* | Patrick Malahide | *Middlemarch* | Richard Stirling | *Little Dorrit* |
| Tracey Childs | *Howard's Way* | Roy Marsden | *Inspector Dalgliesh* | David Suchet | *Poirot* |
| Nula Conwell | *The Bill* | John McArdle | *Brookside* | John Thaw | *Morse* |
| Nicholas Courtney | *Dr Who* | Sylvester McCoy | *Dr Who* | Daniel J Travanti | *Hill Street Blues* |
| Pauline Daniels | *Brookside* | Joe McGann | *The Upper Hand* | Susan Twist | *Brookside* |
| Stefan Denis | *Neighbours* | Mark McGann | *The Hanging Gale* | Don Warrington | *Rising Damp* |
| Gary Files | *Neighbours* | Paul McGann | *The Hanging Gale* | Marcia Warren | *Dangerfield* |
| Bridgit Forsyth | *The Likely Lads* | | *The Monocled Mutineer* | Tom Watson | *EastEnders* |
| William Gaunt | *The Champions* | Steve McGann | *The Hanging Gale* | Benjamin Whitrow | *Pride and Prejudice* |
| Jan Graveson | *EastEnders* | Ian Ogilvy | *The Saint, Shoestring* | Paula Wilcox | *Please Sir* |

And so on to a few of the names of well known performers, who don't get a mention elsewhere in this volume, but they called in to the Playhouse on their way up to fame and fortune – or maybe it was on the way down!
True Repertory Company members are indicated with [*]

Francesca Annis 1992
Peggy Ashcroft 1974
Al (Hunter) Ashton 1984
Tony Booth [*]
Peter Bowles 1996
Eleanor Bron 1979
Peter Byrne 1993
Cheryl Campbell 1997
George Chakiris 1992
Nigel Davenport 1990
Alan Dobie 1981, 92
Shelagh Fraser 1977, 79
Brenda Fricker 1980
Penelope Keith 1968
Yaphet Kotto 1990
Ian Lavender 1969
Rosemary Leach [*] 1967
George Melly 1971, 78, 85
Hayley Mills 1995
Warren Mitchell 1980
Derren Nesbitt 1993
Kate O'Mara 1994
Susan Penhaligon 1995
Diana Rigg 1993
Alexei Sayle 1985
Alison Steadman 1985
Sylvia Syms 1992
Denis Waterman 1996
Timothy West 1980

## Chapter Six
## ROMANCE, ROYALTY, LOYALTY, LANDLADIES AND FAITHFUL FRIENDS

One effect of long term close proximity in a rep company is the delight or frustration of that delicious commodity called back-stage romance. Most actors wonder how they ever found time to fall in love, considering the daily routine, starting at 9.30am with rehearsals, which often lasted until 5.30pm, with only a short lunch break. Then the evening call of 6.55pm for a 7.30pm curtain. With the evening not over before eleven, most speak of weariness as the abiding memory of their time in rep.

Stanley Williams, the call boy working in the theatre during the period of 1934 to 1938, remembers that some of the actors slept in the theatre, sprawled out on old settees and armchairs and he would have to wake them up as his first duty upon arrival in the Green Room. His clear memory of the layout of the Green Room at that time, of the Theatre as a whole, of local favourites such as the Belmont Pub, was more than just useful in the preparation of this volume.

The Belmont, next door to the Playhouse, was often known as the 'Outside Green Room', but its name actually came from *The Merchant of Venice* and its rooms were divided by stained glass screens depicting Shakespearean characters. The proprietor, Peter Callan, was referred to by Maud Carpenter as 'the little man in the drinking place', according to his daughter Anne Callan. Anne also remembers Inigo Jackson sitting in the pub, learning his lines for *Luther* whilst eating a sandwich and drinking his beer.

In retrospect, Stanley Williams now realises that he had a wonderful privilege – that of seeing at first hand the courtship of one of the most famous theatre couples this century, Michael Redgrave and Rachel Kempson. It is known that Rachel proposed to Michael, because he hesitated on account of not earning as much as his sweetheart and that at the time of their wedding, the audience laughed, until it stopped the show, because in one scene Michael had to go down on his knees and ask for her hand in marriage. The wedding, at Thurstaston, was recalled by several ladies who, as Brownies, went to see their hero and heroine wed. One of them, the former Mary Aitchison, recalls Rachel's beautiful white wedding gown. When asked if she ever spoke with the Redgraves, she replied that they were all too much in awe of any of the actors, to actually speak to them. She says they stood in the churchyard, watching from a distance.

*"William Lucas and Rowena Ingram slipped away from rehearsals to be married: were back in time for curtain up at the theatre where they play leading roles in, The Love of Four Colonels. But yesterday their secret was out – and it was champagne for two."*
['Liverpool Daily Post', April 1954]

Robert James and Mona Bruce, as well as William Fry and Elsie Lloyd, are also recorded as having slipped away to marry between a matinee and evening show. The most recent to be blessed on stage – Andy Gale and Carrie-Ann Stevens.

Courtship is often observed, but the wedding happens when the actors move on to other venues, as was the case with Moray Watson when he became engaged to Pamela Marmont [daughter of Percy Marmont, an earlier member of the Rep Company].

Roger Philips always thanks Kate Fitzgerald and the Playhouse for the fact that it was during the run of *Kissing Frogs* in 1982 that he went to an after-show party at Kate's place and met her friend Margaret. Now happily married to Margaret and with a family, he makes no secret of his gratitude. Sharon Mughan [Maughan] and Trevor Eve [who later played Shoestring] seemed to do a great deal of their courting at the Playhouse. Trevor became a familiar face as he pursued his lady love. Plenty of the public, seeing him about, apparently kept hoping he would join the Company. Patrick Mower was slightly more circumspect about the beautiful lady from the Box Office who had attracted his attention. Now happily married and with two children, they live abroad in the sunshine of the Mediterranean.

**Other much remembered occasions were the weddings of:**

Cecil Parker and Muriel Randall

Robert Flemying and Carmen Sugars

Antony Hawtrey and Marjory Clark

Richard Briers and Anne Davies

Ivan Stafford and Anne Godley

Malcolm Reid and Helena de Crespo

David Suchet and Sheila Ferris

Sarah Lewis and Paul Gibson

Helen Lindsay and Alan Pikford

Brian Miller and Elizabeth Sladen

*Michael Redgrave and Rachel Kempson outside the theatre in 1936. [Stanley Williams' collection]*

**Opposite** *Richard Briers and Ann Davies at their 1957 wedding at St Nicholas Church Liverpool.*

THE PLAYHOUSE
LIVERPOOL
1911 GOLDEN JUBILEE 1961
THE CHAIRMAN, THE LORD COHEN OF BIRKENHEAD,
AND THE DIRECTORS, CORDIALLY INVITE
MISS M. TICKLE
TO BE PRESENT AT A GALA PERFORMANCE AT THE PLAYHOUSE,
WILLIAMSON SQUARE, ON SATURDAY NOVEMBER 4TH 1961, AT 5.30 P.M.
WHEN "THE SCHOOL FOR SCANDAL" BY R. B. SHERIDAN WILL BE PRESENTED
DINNER JACKETS
R.C.V.P. TO
THE MANAGER, THE PLAYHOUSE,
WILLIAMSON SQ., LIVERPOOL

*Invitation to the Golden Jubilee Gala Performance of
'School For Scandal' for Miss M Tickle.*

*Opposite HRH Princess Marina, Duchess of Kent
with Lord Cohen and Sir Charles Trustam, a Board
member. In the background is Lady Derby who
acted as hostess to the Duchess when she visited
the Playhouse.*

**The Queen never came**. Who did and who didn't visit The Repertory Company and its beautiful theatre building, is sometimes clouded in false memory. Perhaps some confusion arises because of the close proximity of the Royal Court, or the fact that before the advent of cinema, Liverpool could boast that it had 54 theatres. Certainly some of the over-nineties who helped with this book did, on occasion, get some of their facts muddled. But enough evidence exists to help verify those details that are correct.

Jessie Griffiths, who sadly died just after her 100th birthday in 1997, is a case in point. This lovely lady, a member of the Townswomen's Guild in Bebington, gave much that was true and accurate to our research, save one fact, she was adamant that the Queen came to the Playhouse. Of all the information collected via the help of the Townswomen's Guild, The National Association of Women's Clubs, or from the public response to press and radio appeals, this was the most repeated inaccuracy. Eventually the reason became clear. When Her Majesty the Queen visited the Empire Theatre, the Rep sent a group of actors to perform a short piece, and a picture of the Queen meeting the cast afterwards was published in the Rep's Diamond Jubilee Book. It is the memory of this photograph which seems to be the main culprit in causing this confusion.

There are some muddled memories about Sir John Gielgud, who in fact only came as a frequent member of the audience, – never as performer. When he was appearing at the Royal Court, Maud Carpenter decided that it would be good for the Company to see him. As the two theatres carefully avoided having matinees on the same day, Rosalie Crutchley, amongst others, remembered that Maud, in 1936, lined them up 'two by two' in a school crocodile and marched them between the two theatres with a, "Now, boys and girls!"

**So who were the Royal Guests who graced the front row of the Dress Circle?** The late Princess Marina, Duchess of Kent, in 1951. She is described as looking bored. The only lasting memory of her visit was that the specially refurbished ladies' toilet, at the rear of the Dress Circle, was for many years to be known as 'The Throne' by the regular clientele of the Circle.

In 1961 Katherine, the new Duchess of Kent was sent by the Palace as a minor Royal to grace the Golden Jubilee celebrations. Still new to the game of royalty, she was nevertheless charming when introduced and delighted everyone present. A special platform was erected to allow her to see, and be seen, more clearly. Bill Selby recounted the episode, detailing a rather slip-shod official security inspection taking place at 1.30am on the day in question.

On the day of the investiture of Prince Charles as the 21st Prince of Wales, the Playhouse was performing a *Victorian Music Hall*. For this one occasion, instead of the *National Anthem*, the whole cast sang *God Bless the Prince of Wales*. It brought the house down.

The 1981 Diamond Jubilee guest was Princess Margaret. She did not seem very interested in the *Tale of Two Cities*. Hardly surprising, as she was seated in the front row of the Dress Circle and all Liverpudlians of five foot stature know – never sit in row A of the Dress. A certain sympathy went out to her from those equally challenged with lack of height. The lasting Scouse joke on the matter is that she probably went home and told her almost equally short sister not to go to the Rep "… as you won't see over the top of the barrier!"

After that the Board lost interest in trying to up-market themselves via Royalty. It had been made abundantly clear that they were not going to get Royal status. Liverpool had a Royal Court, it didn't need a Royal Liverpool Playhouse.

*John Franklyn-Robbins in 'Peer Gynt', directed by Dick Tuckey, 1972. [Loaned by JFR]*

Prince Edward, on the other hand, was considered the most relaxed of the Royals to visit the theatre. When in 1992 the now well-established independent Brouhaha Festival held its second International Festival, under the management of its founder, Kate Willard, Edward, happy in theatrical circles and familiar with the dreams and ambitions of young people in the arts world, was an obvious and successful choice. Although the presentation was good and he enjoyed himself, Prince Edward must have felt as constrained as the performers and audience by the almost paranoid security surrounding the event, brought about by the then threatening Irish question.

One of the most frequently asked questions, after "has the Queen ever visited the Playhouse?", is, "have Lawrence Olivier and Vivienne Leigh ever performed there?" The answer is, they were at the Royal Court, but never at the Rep! Neither are they recorded as ever visiting to see a play at the Playhouse.

**Bums on seats.** Whilst playing Peer Gynt in Dick Tuckey's 1969 production, John Franklyn-Robbins had a vividly remembered put-down from a woman in the front row. The play demanded that John appeared on stage as a youthful Peer Gynt, before progressing to more mature levels. "Guthrie's advice to me on playing Peer: 'Nobody plays all three parts well; you're too old for the first, all right in the second, very good in the third.' In Act One, lying down stage leaning on his elbows, John heard a woman in the front row declare. 'He looks so old!'"

Such comments from the audience can be unnerving. Others come dangerously close to causing that much feared disaster – corpsing. Long-time favourite David Goodland remembers that, during the 1974 *Romeo and Juliet*, the delightful Roy McArthur would regularly let slip his grasp upon his heavy sword and somehow it would descend into the front row. That it was usually during a schools' matinee was, in David's recollection, "One way of keeping them quiet!"

Another impressive silencing of a school audience is remembered by Alan Partington. Michael Gambon, playing the title role in *Coriolanus* opposite Stuart Wilson's Tullus Aufidius, took exception to the noise and on one occasion, "… stopping the performance, he walked down-stage to tell them he wasn't prepared to continue unless they were quiet. We did continue!"

Such seriousness was not expected during Michael Gambon's portrayal of Don Ferolo Whiskerandos in *The Critic*, where his masterly technique of high comedy made it almost impossible for the other actors to control themselves.

*Beryl Williams, a much remembered theatrical landlady.*

*Gary Files, in his pre-'Neighbours' days.*

*Gerald Sim in 'The Affair', 1961.*

Arthur Whybrow, however, was delighted to interact with a schools' audience. The memory is given here verbatim as it is a special favourite with the tour guides at the Theatre.

*"I played the Gravedigger in 'Hamlet'. I know there are supposed to be two, but I think Dick Tuckey thought the second one was superfluous and asked me to amalgamate the lines and just play it as a stand up comic. In Rep, stage staff are fairly responsible as a rule, but do occasionally let off steam with the odd joke. In my case it happened at a schools' matinee. When I climbed into the grave [a hole in the stage], instead of the usual two or three skulls there was a huge pile, in excess of a dozen. Entering into the spirit of the thing, while singing the little ditty the Gravedigger usually sings, I gaily chucked all the skulls out, one by one, to the great enjoyment of the students in the front row. However, I was a little too enthusiastic as at least one rolled off the edge of the apron. I got out, walked down stage and just as if I was asking a neighbour for my ball back, I said to one of the lads in the front row, 'Can I have MY skull back?' Cheap laugh but what the heck! The Gravedigger then goes on into a question and answer bit, usually with the second gravedigger, but in this case I had to do it alone facing the audience. 'What is he that builds stronger than either the mason, the shipwright or the carpenter?' I said out front. I paused, I was just about to give them the answer, when from the circle a lad called out, 'A gravedigger!' The audience totally collapsed with laughter. I waited then said, 'You clever fellow, right – the rest of you, ignorant.' More laughter. [The boy had been right as the script allows the second gravedigger to suggest 'a gallows maker' and then I would have rejoined long-windedly that it was indeed 'a gravedigger'] Meanwhile, in the wings, Hamlet and Horatio were waiting to come on. As they came down, John Castle said to me, quietly, out of the side of his mouth, 'Remind me never to work with you again!' I'm delighted to say he didn't fulfil his threat and we have since worked together."*

Liverpool audiences are renowned for their sensitivity to their own accents and dialects. It can be disconcerting, as Marjorie Yates recalls: "As a very green young actress I played Viola and was horrified in my first matinee scene when I said "So this is Illyria ..." and a chorus of kids in the stalls shouted "Get stuffed, lady!" and threw pennies on the stage. I believe I had spoken the lines in a broad Birmingham accent!"

**Landladies and digs.** If a sailor has a girl in every port, every actor has a landlady story for every town they visit. One aspect of the long-term contract was the saga of differing friendships which grew up between them, the various levels of respect and the nightmares of bad digs.

Robert Donat is reputed as having his first Liverpool digs in an attic room with such a low ceiling he was forced to put his head out of the skylight, in order to do up his tie.

Beryl Williams was the theatrical landlady most remembered from the seventies. Her large house frequently overspilt with thespians to such an extent that some had to sleep in the dining room. Named as 'Jacaranda', the house was papered with pictures from magazines. Gilbert Wynne describes, "… having a single bed tucked into the corner of her dining room; it was like sleeping in the nave of a cathedral." He hastens to add that both Beryl and her husband were very kind to him.

Although better remembered for his part as Tom Ramsey in the Australian soap opera *Neighbours*, Gary Files has happy memories of his time with the Company in 1968. It is Beryl and her family who were the main theme of his letter written for this history.

"Her name was Beryl Williams and I got her name and etceteras off the theatre notice board near the stage door. She was Liverpool Chinese and was married to Alan who was Liverpool Welsh – their son Justin [who must be in his thirties now] was a fascinating mix – as was his accent. Pure Liverpudlian. I enclose a snap of them."

Others recalled the fact that Alan owned the 'Blue Angel' club and had also been involved with the Cavern night club during the Beatles era. It was generally recognised that if one brought back an overnight guest, one should add a little to the rent. The going rate was £1 under the pillow, regardless of the visitor's status and many a relative was bemused by the implications of their stay.

Parts of the area near Beryl's house had a certain reputation and stories abound. Pamela Pitchford says that Huskisson Street, "wasn't very salubrious in those days" and Bryony McRoberts is one who mentions kerb-crawlers appearing if she was walking home alone to the digs. Milton Johns remembers, "… a time during the election, when one of the brothels sported a notice announcing 'Let's Go with Labour', which I thought was rather unfortunate. The girls always asked us how business was – but I could never quite bring myself to return the question."

"Somewhere behind the railway station", is Gerald Sim's recollection of his theatrical digs. "It was winter, very cold, my bed was lumpy beyond belief, but it pummelled into shape eventually. The bath was enormous and the tap very slow. By the time it was three inches deep the water was cold. Not unique of course – digs have always been a lottery."

Michael Poole stayed in a flat in Hope Street, which was decorated with thirteen different wallpaper samples plus picturesque damp patches on the outer walls. He noted that all the best digs were already occupied by more permanent members of the company. When Dorothea Alexander arrived in 1956, Covent Garden Opera Company and its orchestra had filled the available spaces, but Maud Carpenter helped her get a sofa in someone's front room.

'Opposite the Cabbage Patch' were favourite digs for many actors. The famous, colourful and seemingly ageless, 'Rusty' lived above a shop in a mountainous labyrinth of twisting staircases whose walls were adorned with hundreds of photographs of her favourite visitors. She loved coming to Press night parties, dressed in black velvet and masses of jewellery.

Miranda Bell was lucky in being able to stay at the Shaftesbury Hotel. The staff used to make her tea and toast after the theatre, and sit talking, keeping a wary eye open for the manager. Jacqueline Morgan however caps it all: "I don't have any 'landlady' stories as I stayed with my Mum and Dad in Crosby – the best digs in the world."

**The Animal Kingdom.** Superstition made many a performer wary of magpies, or delighted to see a black cat. And working with children or animals has long been regarded as a kiss of death. They take over the stage, they draw the audience's eye away from the adult star, they can ruin your performance. In 1971, Gilbert Wynne recalls an incident with a rat which nearly stopped the performance of *Signpost to Murder*.

"I was standing stage left near the proscenium arch with Neil Cunningham approaching towards me from centre stage. He suddenly looked down to the left of my feet with a look of horror on his face. I thought, 'This is new!' Then I glanced down myself to see a very large rat apparently thoroughly enjoying the play. I looked quickly back at Neil, who was standing speechless; then with a look of great relief; he began to speak. I then of course realised the rat must have become bored and left."

Many people remember Percy, or his relatives. So many, that we could not record them here, but thank you to Margery Tickle of

## Percy joins the cast.

The audience at Liverpool Playhouse gasped last night when Percy, the theatre rat, walked on to the stage towards the end of the current production of Relatively Speaking.

The cast "dried up" temporarily, but Percy was unconcerned and after a look round he scurried off again.

A Playhouse spokesman said to-day: "He is a great friend of ours. We call him Percy. We haven't been able to cast him yet because we can't catch him to find out the name of his agent."

'Percy' press cutting. [Liverpool Daily Post and Echo]

Tybalt the most famous theatre cat. [Loaned by Jackie Bullock]

**Opposite** Michael Malnick with Sim the cat from the 1959 production of 'Visit to a Small Planet', directed by Willard Stoker.

Aintree who was one of the first to do so. On another occasion often recalled by the elderly, one of the rat population calmly walked across the velvet top of the Dress Circle. No mention has ever been made of women screaming or the audience running away. It seemed as if they were all used to them. Arthur Whybrow recalls:

> "One evening I was standing in the wings, when we were doing 'Great Expectations' [he was playing Magwitch]. During one of the scenes showing Miss Haversham's large decrepit run down room, one of the biggest rats I've ever seen walked slowly onto the apron from stage right. He walked about a third of the way across, then sat down and slowly and carefully preened himself. The two girls doing the scene fortunately were focused upon each other and did not see him. Even the audience seemed to give no noticeable reaction. It was as if because Miss Haversham's place was so tatty, they accepted the rat as part of the scene and had presumed it was a trained tame real rat or clever clockwork toy … the animal sat there for perhaps two or three minutes at least before sauntering off stage left. I fully expected an exit round of applause, but no, the audience remained intent upon the spoken word."

There is no doubt that the presence of a livestock market behind the Playhouse had something to do with an increase in vermin during the days before the St John's market was rebuilt. What is not so easily explained is that Percy is a 1971 rat! A possible reason was given in 1998 when, following the closure of the building, rats appeared. The Health Inspector called in said that the heavy rain of 1998 had forced the water table up and there was an increase in sightings of rats. What was the water table doing in 1971?

The Playhouse's most famous theatre cat was Tybalt, named after the quote, "What is Tybalt? More than prince of cats" [*Romeo and Juliet*, act II scene IV]. He lived below stairs at night and during the day, he roamed the theatre, visited the dressing rooms of those who were generous with titbits and then frequently settled on a piece of the set for the rest of the day. Wardrobe Mistress, Liz Horrigan, recalls several incidents which still make her smile. In her day, there was a board on the Wardrobe door, so that messages from the actors could be passed on for running repairs to be dealt with quickly. One day, soon after Tybalt had been neutered, a note was left, "Please take a tuck in Tybalt's back legs!" She also recalls how it was Christopher Bullock who cared for the cat, even coming in on Sundays to feed it. On one occasion, the fire brigade would not let him into the theatre, because of a fire in the adjoining Market. He importuned the poor fireman, who said Chris could have three minutes to find the cat. Chris opened the door and Tybalt leapt out into his arms. Many actors mentioned the cat and the fact that he seemed to sense when a performance was about to take place and would disappear. Tybalt obstinately refused to participate in any show and if a cat was needed, one had to be imported for the occasion.

Sim, Michael Malnick's Siamese, was cast as the cat in *Visit to a Small Planet*, the fun evening show for Christmas 1959/60. Sim had a speaking role, since his owner played the part of an alien who could talk to animals. He had a tendency to build up his part, though, especially during two particularly long soliloquies. It is not recorded how the young Ben Whitrow coped with the cat, but Hilary Crane was apparently a hit with Sim.

Nowadays, dogs are not allowed back stage, but some get away with it. Whenever the likes of Stephanie Laurence or Jenny Seagrove have appeared at the Playhouse, their favourite pet has usually managed to be illiterate where 'keep out' signs are concerned. The truth is most theatre people are a little animal crazy, perhaps because they ease the bruises of insecurity. Sometimes they add to those bruises.

In 1959, in a play called *Speaking of Murder* by Audrey and William Roos and directed by Frederick Farley, the actress Caroline

*Diana Rigg and Tim Woodward with Adam Booth and Mark Arends in 'Medea', directed by Jonathan Kent 1993. [Phil Cutts]*

Blakiston played the part of a secretary plotting to murder her employer's wife. Testing out the chosen method for the deed, the wife's dog is shut up in a large safe, his ensuing death recorded and the play continued. However, several actors have recounted the story of the night when the supposedly dead dog suddenly leapt onto the stage, jumped onto the policeman's lap as he sat on a sofa, and proceeded to lick the young man's face. The audience's laughter was not helped by Dulcie Bowman's hissing from the wings trying to get her lovely spaniel, Oscar to come to her. In the end the policeman, played by Trevor Danby, simply picked up the young rascal and delivered him to the wings. Oscar, listed in the programme as Oscar Bowman, was a familiar sight around Liverpool.

Unfortunately the only photo available of Dulcie Bowman and Caroline Blakiston together on stage is not from *Speaking of Murder*, but from *The Banbury Nose*. That was the debut performance of a young teenager called William Kenwright who appeared alongside them, but we have not found a photograph which records the occasion.

One dog who is not forgotten is Bart, a dog about to be put down in 1957, only to find himself auditioning and winning a part in *A Man About The House* and then hitting the headlines in the *Liverpool Echo*, the local evening paper. Seventy other dogs were immediately rescued from various dog homes as a result of the publicity and Bart was regarded as a real hero. After the run of the play, Bart was adopted and lived happily in his new home.

**That's my Mummy!** From the days of Noel Coward's first appearance, children have shone on the Playhouse stage. Virtually every season has seen at least one play which demanded, even depended upon, the talents of the young. Out front, or on stage, the reactions of children as actors or audience often lends something to the humour of the performance.

Clare Dow, in Ian Kellgren's last production at the Playhouse [*A Christmas Carol*, 1995], had to play several parts, one of them as Mrs Cratchet. All went well until, during the Boxing Day matinee, playing the role of that hard pressed and impoverished character, she was serving up the meagre fare for the family meal. She and most of the front of the audience had to struggle to retain their composure, when from the front row her eighteen-month-old daughter, Colette, began to loudly call out, "That's my Mummy!" Clare was able to laugh off the incident with good humour, saying that, "It must have been the way I was dishing out the potatoes!"

One of the best remembered stories of the 15-year-old Noel Coward is from the dress rehearsal for his first professional appearance, in 1913. All went well, then during the procession of angels and spirits, Noel Coward suddenly stopped walking. He appeared white faced. Asked what was the matter, he replied, "Please may I leave the room?" To this day the chaperone is always reminded, "Come via the loos, please!" Joan Groundsell, the last of a long line of devoted chaperones, was excellent at controlling the nervousness of her young charges.

Marjorie Magee [nee Lowe] recalled the visits made by the Blackburne House girls during the pre-war years. She remembers wearing the bridesmaid's dress she had worn the previous year to her brother's wedding. It was turquoise taffeta and if her memory served her right, she believed it was from C & A Modes. Her other memory, shared by other old girls, was of Miss Ashwell lecturing them on how to behave at the theatre.

To celebrate her Silver Wedding, Marjorie excitedly hired a bus and came with 18 of her old school friends to see *The Complaisant Lover* by Graham Greene [1968]. When asked was her husband with them, she replied, "We did it as we did in the 1930s, all girls together".

*Lisa Walker, Beryl Smith and Carol Walker, three generations of one family who worked in the Front of House. Carol began her career at the Playhouse as an usherette during Leslie Lawton's era and rose to the position of duty manager, where she continued until 3 January 1998.*

Pat Burgess and Beryl Spellman, two members of the Playhouse History Group in the 1990s, recall mothers taking their children to Christmas matinees with large juicy oranges, which the mothers would knead until the flesh inside was loose. They would then insert a straw and the children would drink, much as youngsters do today out of their cardboard cartons.

**Playhouse Circle.** From the very early days, this offstage organisation was formed to provide lectures, discussions and social events for the benefit of regular theatregoers. Their monthly meetings were addressed by some very eminent writers, academics and theatre personalities – AA Milne, Hilaire Belloc, L du Garde Peach, or as already quoted, the likes of St John Ervine. By leading to discussions on the texts being used, a greater understanding of the substance of work by playwrights such as GB Shaw was reached.

**Friends of the Liverpool Playhouse Society.** Their constitution was adopted at a special meeting on Monday 5 June 1978, and following the period of Administration, 1991, was amended at a special EGM on Monday 9 September 1991. During the 'Too Good to Lose' campaign of 1991, when the theatre was under threat of closure, John Stalker, Caroline Bailey and Rebecca Farrar of the theatre staff appealed to the Friends who were at that point very inactive. Subsequently money was made available to the company from the Friends' funds. At the September meeting the decision was taken to revitalise the membership, make its commitment to the support of the theatre more positive and put less stress on the cultural side of the Friends. This in fact made the Friends a more vibrant and positive organisation and brought them into alignment with the fund-raising policies of the company. Although it still pursued the cultural interests of its original constitution, from September 1991 under the leadership of Elizabeth Christie and later Val Strauss and Jean Mills, the Society became a valued machine for supplementing the theatre's income.

**Family connections.** Dynasties abound in thespian circles, like father like son, like mother like daughter! The Redgraves, Sir Michael 1934 – 1935 and Lady Rachel, 1935 – 1936 are supposedly the Liverpool Rep's most famous family, having also seen Vanessa and Corin as guests, and Joely Richardson in her debut in *Miss Julie* in 1985.

The only other three generation association is backstage, when Beryl Smith, her daughter Carol Walker and her granddaughter Lisa Walker, were all employed simultaneously as front of house staff.

Two generations are recorded for the Thorndikes. Eileen Thorndike, 1914, had been followed by her sister, Dame Sybil Thorndike in 1943, Dame Sybil's son Christopher Casson, 1933 – 1934. Interestingly, the son appeared at the Playhouse ten years before his mother arrived, to perform with the Old Vic Company.

The Friends of Liverpool Playhouse 1996 work party, on stage with the author, Pelham McMahon. From top right: Maisie Huckell, Ruth Taylor, Sylvia Laurence, Jan Strong, Wendy Rehill, Lynne Pyne, Fiona Martin, and Jean Mills seated on the right, with Pelham standing. [Anne Gilmore]

## Chapter Seven
# A WORLD OF WORDS AND MUSIC

The nearest accurate figure, after a careful collating of all available records and programme details, gives 917 as the number of playwrights known to have had their work performed at the Playhouse. They provided the material for a total number of nearly two thousand productions. Of those, 229 new works are recorded as premieres, 1932 being the most prolific year with 12 new works listed, including several double bills.

As co-writers, Helen Granville Barker and her husband, Harley Granville Barker, make the top 50 list as a husband and wife team, when their solo work is added to their collaborative work. In reality, Susan Glaspell and Catherine Hayes should stand as the most performed female solo writers. In the male dominated world of writing, the first woman to have her play performed by the Rep was Elizabeth Robbins with *Makeshift* [1914].

Of the 917 playwrights, less than ten per cent are recorded as female writers, but there are several writers whose name appears only once and who use initials to identify themselves. It is almost impossible to clarify the situation.

It took thirty-six years, for someone as young as 20 to have a work put on at the Liverpool Playhouse. Sydney Jeffery's notes, donated to the Archives by the Jeffery family, make the comment that Lionel Hale's play, *She Passed Through Lorraine*, made him the youngest author produced thus far. The actual youngest from all plays is not known, as some of the Youth Theatre productions were definitely written by teenagers. Scott Williams is recorded as 18 years of age when he wrote *Growing Young*.

Actors writing plays is not unknown, the most famous from the Playhouse being Lynda Marchal, now better known as Lynda la Plante. Michael Redgrave also wrote plays and *The Seventh Man* was premiered on 8 May 1935. In December 1935 *Circus Boy*, also by Redgrave, was the Christmas show for that year. In *Circus Boy* there appeared a "Miss Patricia Hayes from London, who, although young, has attained some fame as a boy impersonator." [Press cutting book] She was later famous as *Edna, the Inebriate Woman* and as Alf Garnett's neighbour.

In June 1996, a distinguished cast headed by Daniel J Travanti of *Hill Street Blues* fame, Hannah Gordon, and Moira Lister appeared in a revival of Michael Redgrave's version of *The Aspern Papers*. Best described as a wordy script, by 1990s standards, it nevertheless was popular with many because of the obvious skill of the leading ladies.

Of the 171 writers who have only one production to their credit, William Hywel should not be ignored. His play, *The Bonesetter of Crosshall Street*, was an inspiration to all who attended and a triumph for Lord Cohen who had encouraged its presentation. Few people today will remember that techniques for the successful setting of broken bones were developed in Liverpool. With a cast which included Peggy Mount, Cyril Luckham, Manning Wilson and Eric Lander, it was reviewed by Walter George as, "Cyril Luckham dominated in this play as he does in so many. It was one of the high spots in Gerald Cross's period as Director." The play had a particular interest for Liverpool in that William Hywel was, in fact, Doctor William Hywel Jones, a descendant of the bone-setting pioneer, Evan Thomas of 1854. The play followed the life of Evan Thomas, who was subject to abuse as a quack in the early part of his career, but emerged as a leading exponent in his field. Out of this wonderful family emerged the now famous Sir Robert Jones, the eminent orthopaedic surgeon. Interestingly, Sidney Jeffery notes, "It was calculated, as local history, to interest Liverpool" [Page 31 Journal Number 5]. The local story-line appealed to a wide local base and showed Liverpool in a good light, a popular feature with the Rep audiences.

Local writing has consistently proved popular. Affection might, on some occasions, appear to supersede quality, but loyalty is at its best when responding to what is home grown. Plays billed as intended for London or more universal markets have, on occasion, not been well received by the canny Playhouse subscriber.

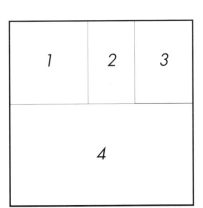

*Montage of all the Shirleys. [1] Noreen Kershaw, 1986 [Everyman, World Premiere]. [2] Paula Wilcox, 1992. [3] Kate Fitzgerald,1991. [4] Pauline Daniels, 1996. [Phil Cutts]*

## Popular Playwrights

171 writers had one production
646 had two, three or four productions
76 had five to nine productions
24 had ten or more productions

The most produced playwright each decade
1911 – 1919 **George Bernard Shaw** 10 productions
1920 – 1929 **JM Barrie** 13 productions
1930 – 1939 **Philip Johnson** 13 productions
1940 – 1949 **William Shakespeare** 11 productions
1950 – 1959 **William Shakespeare** 11 productions
1960 – 1969 **William Shakespeare** 8 productions
1970 – 1979 **William Shakespeare** 13 productions
1980 – 1989 **Willy Russell** 9 productions
1990 – 1998 **John Godber** 9 productions

Most performed writers
1 **Shakespeare** 57 productions of 22 plays
2 **Shaw** 49 productions of 26 plays
3 **Barrie** 32 productions of 18 plays
4 **Galsworthy** 25 productions of 19 plays
5 **Chekhov** 19 productions of 8 plays
6 **Maugham** 18 productions of 13 plays
7 **Coward** 17 productions of 12 plays
8 **Philip Johnson** 17 productions of 17 plays
9 **Priestley** 17 productions of 13 plays
10 **Ibsen** 16 productions of 10 plays

Apart from Shakespeare, each decade was dominated by the most popular writers of the day. The breakdown is as follows:

1911 – 1919 **Shaw** 10 **Galsworthy** 9 **HH Davies** 8 **Barrie** 7 **Jeans** 7 **Wilde** 7 **Shakespeare** 4
1920 – 1929 **Barrie** 13 **Galsworthy** 11 **Brighouse** 10 **Shaw** 10 **Milne** 8 **Shakespeare** 5
1930 – 1939 **Philip Johnson** 13 **Priestley** 9 **Barrie** 7 **Shakespeare** 6 **Bridie** 5 **Rice** 5
1940 – 1949 **Shakespeare** 11 **Shaw** 8 **Chekov** 6 **Bridie** 4 **Ustinov** 4
1950 – 1959 **Shakespeare** 11 **Shaw** 6 **Fry** 4 **Stoker** 4 **Settle** 4
1960 – 1969 **Shakespeare** 8 **Shaw** 6 **Coward** 4 **Osborne** 4
1970 – 1979 **Shakespeare** 13 **Ayckbourn** 7 **Bleasdale** 5 **Willis Hall** 5 **Shaw** 5 **Tuckey** 5
1980 – 1989 **Russell** 9 **Catherine Hayes** 5 **Jim Morris** 5 **Bleasdale** 4 **Shakespeare** 3 **Debbie Horsfield** 3 **Bill Morrison** 3 **Stoppard** 3
1990 – 1998 **Godber** 9 **Russell** 6 **Dave Simpson** 3 **Shakespeare** 2

Most performed or the top ten plays
1 *Twelfth Night* 9 productions
2 *She Stoops to Conquer* 6 productions
3 *Macbeth* 6 productions
4 *Candida* 5 productions
5 *Uncle Vanya* 5 productions
6 *Present Laughter* 5 productions
7 *Shirley Valentine* 5 productions
8 *Midsummer Night's Dream* 5 productions
9 *School for Scandal* 5 productions
10 *The Importance of Being Earnest* 5 productions

Production totals for the most popular writers over the 86 year period.

Shakespeare 63 [including 6 exerpts] GB Shaw 50
JM Barrie 32 J Galsworthy 25 A Chekov 19
WS Maugham 18 Noel Coward 17 Philip Johnson 17
JB Priestley 17 H Brighouse 16 H Ibsen 16 AW Pinero 16
Willy Russell 15 AA Milne 14 St John Ervine 13
H Granville Barker 13 Ronald Jeans 13 Oscar Wilde 12
Alan Bleasdale 11 James Bridie 11 RB Sheridan 11
Alan Ayckbourn 10 Alan Bennett 10 Willis Hall 10
HH Davies 9 John Godber 9 F Lonsdale 9 Alfred Sutro 9
Samuel Beckett 8 HA Jones 8 Arthur Miller 8
Peter Ustinov 8 Mrs Granville Barker 7 John Osborne 7
Elmer Rice 7 R Settle [Musicals] 7 Antony Tuckey 7
Keith Waterhouse 7 Christopher Fry 6 Susan Glaspell 6
Oliver Goldsmith 6 Catherine Hayes 6 Bill Naughton 6
Neil Simon 6 Willard Stoker 6

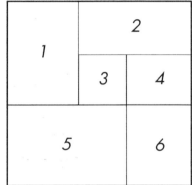

| 1 | 2 | |
|---|---|---|
| | 3 | 4 |
| 5 | | 6 |

Some of the writers whose work has graced the Playhouse stage. [1] Hugh Walpole. [2] Alan Bleasdale. [Liverpool Daily Post and Echo] [3] Catherine Hayes. [4] Jim Hitchmough, [Phil Cutts] [5] Willy Russell. [Phil Cutts] [6] Paul Goetzee.

One of the most important local writers to have work in the Playhouse Studio was Jim Hitchmough with his first presentation of *Watching*, later taken up and produced as a Granada TV serial. A large circle of local writers vied for the position of Writer-in-Residence. One of the first was Pat Anderson, who still writes and lectures in Liverpool. She was followed by Andrew Cullen, who won 'Playwright of the North' and whose first play at the Playhouse was *North* in May 1989. In September 1992, Andrew Schofield appeared in Cullen's *Self Catering*; his memory of him is as a very quiet man, very meticulous and very clever, whose work was directed by Kate Rowland in the Studio. A story about the survival of the fittest, it was promoted by Alan Bleasdale and produced as a TV play for Channel 4.

Other writers included Shaun Duggan, with *A Brusque Affair* [directed by Kate Rowland] in May 1989. Shaun went on to write for *Brookside*. And Scott Williams, with *Growing Young* 1989 and *Get Another Lover, Mother* 1993 [Kate Rowland]. Scot is now a writer and actor.

Kate Rowland went on to work for the BBC as a producer, but was instrumental in supporting and promoting, if not directing, many seasons of new work at the Playhouse Studio, not least that of 1995 which saw the arrival of Phyllis Nagy's *Weldon Rising*.

1995 saw Richard Gardiner directing *Luck of the Draw* by Pelham McMahon for the Applecore Theatre Company and in the same year Ramin Gray directed *Harry's Bag*, by Stephen Butchard, who is now writing for TV. This was followed by *Pig's Ear* written by Andrew Cullen. Meanwhile Liam Lloyd wrote and produced *The Tangled Web* following his period of Writer in Residence. Sadly, the support offered to this writer was limited as funding became more difficult.

Paul Burn had been noted in the late 1980s and early 1990s for the studio productions of his work, some with local history themes. The most notable was *Archangel*, the story of a murder in Aigburth around the turn of the century, which Joe Riley described as, "A fascinating piece of local history, entertainingly told". After this, Paul was invited on to the readers' panel at the Playhouse. Many scripts were sent in to the Playhouse, by aspiring writers and a team of readers was constantly used by the Artistic Directors to assist in this work. Script reports which indicated some promise sometimes had a second reading, before getting to the Director himself. Paul Goetzee of Liverpool Lunchtime Theatre and Fred Lawless of the Liverpool Playwrights, were just two of the team during the later years. The work of both men was much admired by Richard Williams, but they also became victims of the Playhouse's lack of cash for new works. Fred Lawless luckily found an outlet for his talent via The Liverpool Playwrights, and the TAPS company for which he was short-listed as Writer of the Year for his play *Near Enough to Touch* about the sinking of the submarine *Thetis*. The BBC Radio picked up on this new work and it was broadcast nationally to great acclaim.

Fred was also instrumental in presenting the various Liverpool Summer Festivals of Comedy, at the Playhouse. These events also showcased early work from the likes of Karen Brown [now writing for the BBC], Len Prentin [local commissions], Tony Furlong and Jim Powell both of whom went on to develop their play *Night Collar* which finally re-appeared on the main stage in 1998. Originally directed by Marie Higham, the play has remained a favourite with all the Liverpool taxi drivers. Other writers showed an independence and persistence which has to be admired. Tony Bryan who wrote and produced *99 Heywood Street*, using the Studio for its 1992 premiere, was typical of the local writers who used the space to hone their product before taking it on elsewhere.

*'Luck of the Draw' by Pelham McMahon, 1995 directed by Richard Gardiner with Caroline Woodruff, Marie Higham and Helen Wingrave. [Anne Gilmore]*

**Opposite** *Michael Poppins in Harry's Bag by Stephen Butchard and directed by Ramin Gray, 1995. [Phil Cutts]*

Politically contentious drama has not been missing from the repertoire of the theatre. The first is recounted in the Grace Wyndham Goldie book as follows:

"... *The Riot Act* by James Sexton [1913]. The latter was the secretary of the National Union of Dock Labourers. And the play, though in many ways crude, was highly interesting in that it was the first attempt to produce in the theatre a comment on Liverpool life written by a Liverpool author. It dealt with the Liverpool strike of 1911. In this the author had acted an important part. Here were the events, negotiations and characters as he saw them. Enormous interest was aroused in the town; men outnumbered women in the audience; dockers crowded the gallery. The author was much criticised, less for the quality of the play than for the sentiments he expressed. And he held a meeting in the town to defend his attitude. His most determined critics were the suffragettes. The one woman character lied, was disloyal, had a 'past,' made open love to her employer, – and was a suffragette. Here, it was alleged, was an attack upon the whole movement. So suffragettes rose in the stalls, protested and were forcibly ejected; or they addressed the audience from the boxes and were ejected from there."

Apparently these commotions were nothing like the violent, loud and crude behaviour from the audience when, in 1913, they expressed their disapproval of *The Playboy of the Western World* by Synge. Police were brought in to control the audience and the play was taken off within three days. When the 1964 production was put on there was never so much as a murmur.

A Youth Theatre Production brought the pickets out in 1995. The play, a devised piece about teenage pregnancy, *Let's Talk Sex*, was picketed to such an extent that plain clothes police visited it to assess the situation. Later, making themselves known to the theatre management, they asked the age of one performer. She was found to be fifteen and had used a swear word. The censorship was not of the swear word, only of the fact that a minor had used it in a public place. A far cry from the days of the 'Watch Committee,' which, in 1914, complained that the theatre might lose its licence if it did nothing about a section of a play entitled *The Call*, which contained a description of a love affair.

Indeed, getting the permission of the Lord Chamberlain was an important aspect of preparation for the presenting of new work. One impressive story concerning Maud Carpenter comes from just such an incident when William Armstrong had forgotten to apply for a licence for a new play, so he sent Maud to London to see the Lord Chamberlain. She talked her way in to see him and left him the play to read, arranging to come back two hours later. She spontaneously filled in the time by going to see Nelson King about alterations to the script for the children's Christmas show. All went well with both items of business so, before boarding the train home, she sent a telegram to William Armstrong, which arrived during rehearsal. In his excitement he read it out to the full Company, "SEEN KING. ALL IS WELL. MAUD." Believing she had been to Buckingham Palace, the Company went to meet her at Lime Street Station, bearing flowers.

### The Critics. From Doran Godwin, in *Miss Julie* in the Studio in 1976.

"Our first night, full house and the joy and nerves of sharing our production with an audience following weeks of enjoyable rehearsal. During the first act, I could hear this really strange noise in the audience. At the first opportunity, I asked my two fellow actors could they hear it – yes! Was it the wind through the double doors, someone bored or being ill? I said I thought it sounded like someone snoring loudly. Front of House were alerted, and during the final act the problem was dealt with. After the show, I asked what the problem had been and, guess what? It was someone snoring loudly, and that someone was a well-known critic from a national newspaper. I was furious, especially when told that he was, at that very moment, phoning in his crit to the paper.

*'Playboy of the Western World' by JM Synge directed by David Scase, 1965 with Anthony Hopkins, Marjorie Yates and Cynthia Grenville.*

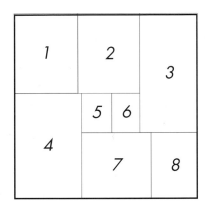

Local media support for the theatre: [1] Colin Voake of BBC Radio Merseyside and 'The Talking Newspaper For The Blind'. [2] Sidney Jeffery, 45 years at the 'Liverpool Daily Post and Echo'. [3] Phil Key of the 'Liverpool Daily Post and Echo'. [4] Roger Philips of BBC Radio Merseyside. [5] Bob Azurdia of BBC Radio Merseyside. [6] Angela Heslop of BBC Radio Merseyside. [7] Joe Riley of the 'Liverpool Daily Post and Echo'. [8] Marjory Bates Murphy of 'The Stage and TV Today'.

*That was too much for me – how could he have an opinion on our production when he had slept through most of it? So I accosted him when he had finished his phoning and all he said was, 'Wait till you read my review!' It was the sort of crit any production would die for, it was wonderful. Friends phoned from all over, having read it the next day – I don't think I have ever had such a glowing crit before or since. Imagine having to tell the truth: 'Yes, the review is marvellous, but the critic snored all the way through: how would he know?'"*

This story has since comforted many a young actor who believed that a critic was not paying attention, and gave meaning to many a director's sarcastic remark "I hope the critic is asleep!"

One thing is quite certain, Colin Voake never slept through a performance. Campbell Mackintosh, one of the editors/writers on the Wirral Talking Newspaper, recalls how Colin, a former teacher and lecturer who became the theatre critic for the local BBC radio, would immediately after seeing a production make his way, firstly to the BBC to record his review, then arrive about midnight at the Mackintosh's and drink a hot cup of Ovaltine as he recorded a review for the Wirral Talking Newspaper. Colin died on 6 January 1988 at about 58 years of age. The tributes given of him by Campbell Mackintosh and Peggy Cool describe him as a brilliant, talented and humble man ... "His style of writing was unique to himself, his voice projection was quite remarkable". Peggy added, "He could make me spellbound, so that I forgot the time!"

Sidney Jeffery has been mentioned several times in this book and his many notes on productions seen at the Playhouse and cuttings of his reviews give a portrait of a meticulous man. His hand-written notebooks often contain comments, entered long after the production, which clarify his original assessment. He seems to have loved making biographical comments, many of which have been useful leads for historical research.

Frequently, big names brought in by Kenwright disappointed the audience by their TV style of performance, which often rendered them almost inaudible, even in a small theatre like the Playhouse. Only in Liverpool would 41 members of an audience walk out on a Peter Hall production – before it got to the interval! They did not like the play and they thought a certain well-known actor was performing badly. Capricious and ungrateful? It maybe a little tongue in cheek, but Doreen Tanner, after 12 years at the *Liverpool Daily Post*, describes the Liverpool audiences in 1974 as, "The Merseyside theatregoer is a touchy creature, always quick to suspect he is being fobbed off with a provincial second best. At the same time he is capable of cold-shouldering the best in the business, if he feels like it ... classic and contemporary work are equally prone to absent audience syndrome. He will ignore the theatre for months on end, then write furious letters to the press about some controversial play, preferably and normally one he hasn't even seen!" Whilst this seems like a caricature, it is more correctly a compliment.

In the local mind's eye, Liverpool was famous for this, 'her Theatre'! Possessiveness appears to be a mark of the Playhouse audience. John Masefield, in his poem written specially for the opening of the Liverpool Repertory Company and recited on stage by Aida Jenoure, acknowledges the theatre's value to the local community. In the mind of the audience, Liverpool Playhouse was the stage which gave them:

'... that one Art
Which is life's inmost soul and passionate heart;
They count the theatre a place of fun
Where men can laugh at nights when work is done.
If it were only that t'would be worthwhile
To subsidise a thing which makes men smile;
But it is more: it is that splendid thing,

A place where man's soul shakes truimphant wing
A place of Art made living, where men see
What human life is and has seemed to be
To the world's greatest brains: it is the place
Where Shakespeare held the glass to Nature's face;
The place the wise Greeks built by public toll
To keep austere and pure the city's soul:

**Music and musicals.** Since the beginning, music has played a part in Rep performances. The first significant Musical Director was Joseph Smith who, with a group of musicians, many of whom had day jobs elsewhere, provided nightly orchestral interludes before, during and after performances, until the Second World War. Joseph Smith's task of matching music to the ethos of the drama, only served to highlight his classical background. He was a man of distinguished appearance and much admired by the ladies. The orchestra pit could accommodate up to sixteen musicians, depending upon the size of the instruments required. A circle of regular musicians made the different ensembles easy to arrange, and live music seems to have been an important feature at the Playhouse. Many programmes list the works to be performed.

During the Second World War, to quote Sydney Jeffery: "It was Sir Tyrone Guthrie who, during this occupancy, [The Old Vic Company] first appointed Ronald Settle as Music Director in 1944. Settle settled!" Ronald Settle played mostly piano. At the second grand piano he was joined by Thomas Haines and later by Joan Ovens. The duets, many arranged by Settle himself, were carefully chosen by him to enhance the mood of the evening and were played before the performance, during the interval and at the end as the audience left the theatre. Ronald Settle composed music for many productions, particularly in collaboration with Willard Stoker in end-of-season revues between 1951 and 1962. The National Anthem was also played at the start of each performance, a tradition which was discontinued in 1965.

A notable operetta was *The Two Bouquets* by Eleanor and Herbert Farjeon, with Victorian songs arranged by Ernest Irving and Ronald Settle [1952]. Sydney Jeffery's opinion of the leading players was that, "... as can scarcely ever be said, six roles were rendered perfectly by Bernard Warwick and Rosamond Burne, as the venerably frisky Papa Gill and Mama, a dragon for decorum; Hugh Paddick, a genius of drollery, as their flirtatious son Edward; Valerie Miller as their sweet-voiced daughter Kate; Robert James as Julian, her sorely-tried suitor; and Manning Wilson as George, the carmine-nosed actor devoted to the bottle."

Another member of the cast of *The Two Bouquets* was that wonderful character actor, Bernard Cribbins. He had been brought over by Willard Stoker from Oldham, where he thought he had been doing quite well, but he modestly tells a tale against himself:

*"It was my very first musical and it was a great joy to do it. It's such a long time ago, but one thing that stands out particularly in my mind was one song I had, about which, on one particular evening, the MD and I had a bit of a battle. He started off, or the band gave me the introduction, and I started in a totally different key. I went all the way through the song and I never deviated from my key and he, of course, couldn't deviate from the key he was in. And we went right through it with him looking heavenwards and waving his arms about frantically and me thinking 'Something's wrong, the band's wrong, of course!' But we somehow got through it. The very next day, I was called to a rehearsal by Willard. I was cut from the song completely. It was taken away and given to the gentlemen of the chorus. He very cleverly let the chorus sing the song to me, or should I say, at me. Sending me up and all I had to do was to respond with a few 'funnies and things' and the whole thing was so much better."*

Despite any such mishap, the production was so well received that it was revived in November of the same year, when a change in the chorus line introduced newcomer, Patricia Routledge. The impresario Baron Vivian saw this show, and restaged it as a Coronation Year attraction in the West End, directed by Willard Stoker and starring Hugh Paddick, where it ran for 228 performances.

*On stage rehearsal of the 1963 production of 'The Entertainer' by John Osborne, directed by David Scase. Frederick Stokes as Archie Rice on stage with David Collins, Ronnie Settle the Musical Director, Joan Ovens and Tony Colgate in the orchestra pit.*

Another memory of Ronnie Settle was included in the large selection of stories from Alan Partington:

"There was a wonderful season of plays to follow and I especially remember Meredith Edwards coming to guest direct 'Under Milk Wood' and play once more the part he originally created in the West End production. His son, Ioan Meredith, played the part of the narrator. I was only down on the cast list as Butcher Beynon but I also played Mr Waldo, who propped up the bar and sang a naughty little number about 'sweeping a young woman's CHIMBLEY' – the things those Welshmen get up to! There was I, boyo, not knowing a thing about all those little dots jumbled about in amongst those four lines. But was I downhearted? No! Ronnie Settle and Joan Ovens … were always on hand to assist with any musical problems – Ronnie always seemed to have a fag end puffing from his mouth and a whole repertoire of amusing stories to break up the seriousness of those music lessons."

**A memory from Caroline Blakiston.** "In 'The Last of Mrs Cheyney', I was seated at the piano, miming a piece, in a scene with Harvey Ashby. Ronnie Settle was hidden behind a 'flat', playing the piano live. He obviously became engrossed in the music. Harvey came to the piano to lift my hands at the same moment as usual, but Ronnie continued to play, so I had to withstand Harvey's efforts. We were running out of dialogue – what to do? With about one line left before the close of the scene, Ronnie suddenly realised his mistake and stopped playing, and I was able to dash to the door in silence to make my exit."

**Memories from Ronald Settle himself are taken from the taped interview in Colin Voake's collection.** "Some nights we have a very quiet audience, who we feel are really listening. Other times, we have a noisy house and we can hardly hear ourselves playing; on such occasions, I sometimes wonder if it is worth the trouble – until I remember that I have received over 500 letters during my time at the Playhouse.

Looking back over my years at the Playhouse I realise that my job has been made more interesting by the fact that all the producers I have worked with have been very fond of music and enthusiastic about its invaluable aid to the art of the theatre. I would mention in particular John Fernald who, in his three years in Liverpool, always displayed the utmost interest in the music. It is probably not known to the theatre-going public that for his production of 'King Lear' he turned composer. Urged by a frenzied desire to compose the numerous trumpet fanfares, he coerced me into committing them to manuscript. Naturally they were complicated and Mr Fernald, having no knowledge of musical notation, transmitted his fanfares to me by means of singing them in a stentorian voice remarkably devoid of true intonation, supplemented by writing them in a form of musical shorthand that had to be seen to be believed. Let it be placed on record, however, that they were extremely effective 'on the night'.

Finally a word about where we live. Many times I have been asked, 'Where do you go when you're not playing?' I think some people imagine that Miss Ovens and I sit huddled in the orchestra pit until the lights go up on the next interval. This is not so. We have our own room, which connects with the door to the orchestra pit and is also adjacent to the iron spiral staircase leading to the OP side of the stage. To me, it is the best room in the theatre, for it is the one which seems to have the most atmosphere. Although for seventeen years there has not been any 'band', it is still called the 'Band Room' – just as it was in the days before Basil Dean produced his first play in 1911. I understand that it was still the Band Room when the Playhouse was the 'Star' [1897], and before that again in the days of the Star Variety [1866]. It is fully and comfortably furnished with possibly the most attractive

*Caroline Blakiston and Harvey Ashby in 'The Last of Mrs Cheyney' by Frederick Lonsdale, directed by Willard Stoker, 1959.*

'Only the Lonely', written by Jon Miller and Shirlie Roden with Larry Branson, the Canadian Roy Orbison look-a-like, in the leading role during 1993 and 1994. It was produced by Bill Kenwright; who shared the directing with Ian Kellgren. As with other Kenwright Productions begun at the Playhouse, this production went on to a successful national tour. It returned to the Playhouse twice more, on the last occasion in 1995 with Peter Howarth in the leading role, because Larry Branson's work permit and home commitments had forced him to leave the show. [Phil Cutts]

**Opposite** The last Musical Director, Steven Markwick, 1997. [Anne Gilmore]

*decor in the theatre, and on its walls are signed photographs of many famous musicians, including Clara Butt, Tetrazzini, Cortot, Pachmann, Kreisler and Sir Thomas Beecham. The unique crescent-shaped table has a sentimental value for me. On it, many famous actors in the Old Vic days [and since] have joined us in games of poker and pontoon – with their eyes on the cards and their ears listening for stage cues. Sometimes, heavily clad in suits of iron, they have cut their entrances very fine, and scampered clangingly up the aforementioned spiral staircase with seconds to spare before they delivered their lines – with one hand deftly concealing a 'running-flush'. It was on the same table that the scores of all the musical plays have been written. I have often thought that if all the famous musicians and now-famous actors who have visited us in the Band Room had signed their names on the walls, it would indeed have become most interesting."*

The great Settle/Ovens partnership was brought to an end in 1972 through financial considerations and changing musical standards. The production immediately following was designed by David Cockayne, and at the request of Antony Tuckey a cover was made for the pit. People remarked that it had a rake which gave it the appearance of a coffin.

During the 1991 financial crisis, James Rushworth, the former Chairman of the Board, provided matching grand pianos for a lunch time fund-raising recital by Ronnie Settle and Joan Ovens. The skill of the pianists was impressive, in spite of the long gap since they had last appeared together, it was a nostalgic event and was very moving.

Much missed by those who enjoyed the music, Joan Ovens seemingly was always in the shadow of the colourful Settle. Her unflappability was legendary and when one evening Ronald Settle collapsed at the piano, Joan continued to play as Bill Selby leapt over the barrier to see to the near unconscious Ronnie. Joan went on to a successful career as a pianist and teacher.

Since 1972 recorded music has occasionally been used for some of the productions, but this was not totally unknown in earlier days – for instance, the programme for *The Witch* by John Masefield, in April 1929, states: "The Church Organ and other effects are by Cinevox, the gramophone record and electrical amplifier, kindly lent by the inventor, WR Mildenstein, of 66 Mount Street."

**Keith Strachan, Musical Director and arranger for Bill Kenwright.** A composer and performer with extensive work in live theatre and on television. He was introduced to the Playhouse by Ian Kellgren and worked on many of the musicals produced by Kellgren and Kenwright. A quiet man, he was popular with everyone at the Playhouse, all of whom respected his talent. Later his son Matthew occasionally came up to assist the Company. [Keith was the composer and co-writer of *The Little Match Girl*, in the 1986 HTV production, which was nominated for an Emmy Award. *Mistletoe and Wine* from this show, recorded by Cliff Richard, gave Keith the 1988 Ivor Novello Award for the best-selling A-side of 1988.]

**Patrick Dineen.** As resident musician, sponsored by Pilkingtons, his work is remembered as innovative and yet surprisingly sensitive to the action of the script. He worked on the music for *Madam Mao* and for *The Fears and Miseries of the 3rd Reich*. As a result of being chosen to attend a masterclass with Stephen Sondheim, Patrick wrote the score for Dostoyevsky's *The Double*, the text of which he adapted and directed, making him the first of the masterclass students to mount a professional production. Much praised, for this and other for studio productions, Patrick has gone on to a successful career as a writer of musicals and of backing music for TV.

Although several names cut across the Bill Morrison / Ian Kellgren / Bill Kenwright seasons which contained various rock and

The December 1996 production of 'Wind in the Willows' with left, Jeffrey Harmer as Badger, Charles Millham as Toad, Damian Gaskin [on the box] as Chief Ferret, Paul Basson front as Mole and to the right, Paul Ryan as Ratty. The set was designed by David Collis as a children's nursery with over large furniture. Lit by David Horn the river bank was created by the use of atmospheric lighting. Directed by Richard Williams, it returned the Playhouse to the tradition of classical drama for children at Christmas. The music was composed by Joanna MacGregor. David Falkner and Joanna Abson accompanied the singing on keyboard and flute. [Phil Cutts]

Tin Man, Scarecrow and the Lion from 'The Wizard of Oz'. The last characters to walk the stage before the Playhouse closed in January 1998, played by Martin Scott Gilmore, Paul Ryan and Mark Bowden. [Liverpool Daily Post and Echo]

roll musicals such as *Be-Bop-a-Lula*, *Good Rocking Tonite*, or *Sergeant Pepper's Magical Mystery Tour*, it is to Andrew Schofield that we turn for some images of that period:

**McMahon** *"'Cavern of Dreams by Carol Ann Duffy', you played Gene Vincent, was it simply another Beatles thing?"*

**Schofield** *"Yes, but this was before it was trendy to do it, you know the way they have a Beatles thing now, a Convention … It was like a fictitious Merseybeat band, and they go to Hamburg, as a lot of bands did at that time. But it was great to do, we had a hell of a time on that one."*

**McMahon** *"And playing Lennon! Does it affect your image as an actor?"*

**Schofield** *"No, I've never felt restricted. To play music's a joy, and to act as, or to portray, someone who was a hero of mine, it's an honour. Mark [McGann] was brilliant. I went to see Mark do it. He's got a great voice, Mark, you know what I mean! It was hard following him, but I had a go. And Karl Lornie, he does Paul McCartney … Karl, he's a really good musician, a very talented lad as regards music and stuff, and that's what he wants to do. Every time the Beatles Convention comes round he goes into that. I had a good time with Karl in the show 'Sergeant Pepper's Magical Mystery Tour'. I used to come on with bits and pieces of spiel in between the songs, and if someone shouted out, that was a laugh already.*

*'Leon Greene was a great singer. And there's another thing I learnt by these operas, because he was properly trained. He was D'Oyley Carte, he was in 'A Funny Thing Happened on the Way to the Forum' and all this stuff. Anyway, he was a great singer and when you were actually next to him you could feel the air move. I know it sounds a bit silly, but when you are with the fellows who can sing, you can hear the air coming from their chest.*

*I was given singing lessons by Geoffrey Walls. I'm sitting in a room and he's on the piano and saying, 'I want you to make your sinus cavities resonate'. So I was saying, 'Can you show me?' And he was sort of playing this chromatic scale and going [Sings} 'Doh. No-o-o-a-ah, no-o-a-a-h' and he was really good. 'Could you do that again?' I ask and he does. [Sings] 'No-o-o-a-ah, no-o-a-a-h' and it was really good. 'Could you do that again and I'll catch on and I'll listen?' [Sings] 'Doh! No-o-o-a-ah, no-o-a-a-h – the skull must resonate – No-o-o-a-ah, no-o-a-a-h', and as he was singing his tooth came out, hit the piano and fell on the floor! He went, 'Ignore it, it's a cap! [Sings] No-o-o-a-ah, no-o-a-a-h. Ignore it, it's a cap!' And I was looking for his tooth! Laugh! He taught me a bit about projection in the lessons.*

*I always watched Peter Holmes because he had a great strong voice. He always gave the impression that he was only talking, but if you were on stage with him he actually nearly took your head off. He had a great line in 'Erpingham Camp' which used to nearly bring the house down. After there's been mayhem, rioting in the holiday camp, he used to burst in and say, 'Sir! Your car has been pushed into Experienced Swimmers Only!' I learned a lot from him about projection."*

## Chapter Eight
## THE SKILLS THAT MAKE THE DIFFERENCE

**B**ackstage and off stage – making it all happen. There has always been a certain air of mystery about backstage. Theatre tours whisk the starry eyed past door after door, "That's Stage Management, that the props room, wardrobe maintenance". An endless list of names, a possible awareness of the purpose – but a sense of the realities an impossibility. What glamour is there in scouring second-hand shops for a tin bath, only to find you are obliged to walk from Scotland Road with it on your back? Trevor Danby describes his experience of prop hunting as, "like walking an interminable and shameful plank … I have never heard so many witty observations focused on a tin bath".

By the time of the 1998 closure, there were 9 backstage dressing rooms. Some of them so small that three people each with a straight-back chair meant that the room was overcrowded. The props room, on the second floor, was a great favourite with school parties visiting for educational workshops. The Friends' Fancy Dress Hire room, the original 1966 – 1972 wardrobe store room, seemed to bulge at the seams. (The main wardrobe was moved to Mathew Street.)

The marketing, sales and publicity offices were on the top floor alongside the Production Manager's room. Usage of all these rooms changed over the years and little attention was paid to them from the point of view of the Tours, except for when college students asked to see specific work places, such as the Production Manager's room or the publicity department, which was of interest to media students.

And as they walked the corridors, people often asked about ghosts at the theatre. Depending on the group, the guide would tell of the top hatted gentleman who walked the back of the gallery looking for his daughter. She had run away from home to be an actress. Or the grey lady, who walked the long corridor outside the Studio. She was supposed to be a grand lady wearing a cloak to disguise herself because she had come to the theatre unaccompanied. Or of Elizabeth who, in 1897, really did fall into the orchestra pit and die. She moved the wrong way when the fire iron came down. Elizabeth is believed to have been seen by many people, sometimes just sitting in the front row of the Gallery in A5, or in the back stalls on the bench seat. The last to report a sighting of her was Pauline Daniels in 1996. Children loved embroidering the stories of Victorian manners which incidents of the old days engendered. They loved trying on the costumes and the theatre staff enjoyed receiving their colourful thankyou notes.

However apocryphal the many versions, Elizabeth's actual manner of death was a reality which was seldom given except when doing Health and Safety Tours with older students. That Elizabeth did die, we know for certain, just as we know the truth of other painful experiences recorded in the archives, or sent in with the personal memories of so many of the different actors. Perhaps the one with the greatest potential for tragedy, for an actor, lies in carelessness in the planning and construction of the set. The attention to detail, the need for care and the dangers that can lurk unseen, require a high level of professionalism and team work, with no independent decisions. Whether it is in the design, where accuracy of measurement is the first necessity for safety, [the ratio of the scale of 1:25cm is the standard used throughout], to completion of a set in the workshop, attention to detail is paramount. In 1992 the set for *Blood Brothers* was not entirely constructed at the Playhouse, a fact which Bill Kenwright Ltd came to regret. Similarly the *Medea* set, which is mentioned later, was not a Playhouse set. Quite apart from care over set construction, the workshop and electrical crews had a reputation for organising the on-stage safety of special effects such as pyrotechnics, trap doors and such items as real cars. The most famous car on the Playhouse stage was a 1906 Gladiator owned by Mr Eric Offley of Ellesmere Port. It was silent on stage, the running noise was a tape recording, as too much emission from the exhaust would have put the stage in a

*Joseph Noble in Richard Williams 1996 production of 'A Midsummers Night Dream'. [Phil Cutts]*

'Habeas Corpus' by Alan Bennett and directed
Susan (Sue) Wilson, 1975. From left to right:
Marius Goring, Patsy Trench, Edward Arthur, Anthea
Holloway, David Beckett, Philip Guard and Vanda
Godsell.

complete fog and probably have choked the audience. Not all solutions to technical problems are easily solved, and some are unwittingly caused by circumstances beyond the control of crew members. Of all the known famous accidents, we begin here with the one which was not the fault of construction, but of an independent action by a Company Manager. The events of the 24 September 1975 are here recorded by the very man who nearly lost his life, the actor, David Beckett:

*"I have a less than happy vivid memory of a dress rehearsal for 'Habeus Corpus', directed by Susan Wilson. I played a character called Perdee who tries to commit suicide at the end of each act. At the end of the first half he tries to hang himself and is helped, inadvertently, when the chair he is standing on is removed from under his feet by Muriel Wisteed [Vanda Godsell] who objects to him spoiling the furniture.*

*On the day in question, I had put on my harness which was attached to the rope from which I would hang myself. This was obviously separate from the false noose which hung around my neck. Prior to making my entrance, the Company Manager, [Derek Killeen] checked that everything was OK and noticed the false noose was showing and, without my realising, taped it up to the harness rope. We carried on until we got to the removal of the chair from under my feet – at which point I blacked out and was literally hanging! I guess that half my weight was on the harness rope and half on my neck. The next thing I can remember is lying on stage with a group of ashen-faced actors and stage hands standing around me. An ambulance then took me to hospital for a check up. As I was in shock, I missed that night's performance of 'Trelawney of the Wells' and the Theatre's Artistic Director, Lesley Lawton, stood in for me, whilst I was looked after by William Lucas. Later I heard from the [elderly] actor John Bromley that he thought I was acting the hanging very well, as I managed to protrude my eyes and tongue and was kicking my legs very realistically! I have since met Derek Killeen and we've had a drink and I've forgiven him."*

From such incidents, lessons are learnt by both actors and crews supporting them backstage. More than the front row had to hold their breath, when Peter Birch swept down the ski slope during a performance of a touring production of John Godber's *On the Piste*. The large set, designed by Julie Godfrey, took up nearly the entire space of the stage as it curved from about twenty feet up 'back stage right' then precariously sloping across to 'stage left', before turning to come to rest at floor level just off 'centre stage'.

A magnificent structure! Night after night, Peter swept down and stopped with a swoosh and a flourish. Everyone held their breath, amazed at his speed, and you could hear the gasp as he stopped on the centre stage apron. A mixture of admiration and relief. And then the local Fire Brigade came into carry out a regular check and, fascinated by the structure, they paid particular attention to it. The white cloth, representing the snow on the slope, needed more fireproofing, they said. No problem to the crew, job done, off they went at the end of their day's work. An hour later, Peter innocently awaits his cue, high up in the wings, sets off and: "… The speed was phenomenal, I just could not control it. I don't know how I managed to steer to the centre aisle, I'm just thankful I did!"

Peter's leap off stage to land way up the aisle is still a talking point with those who saw it. By some miracle, he avoided landing on any member of the public. Had he done so, there is no doubt that someone could have been fatally injured. But, true to form, the Liverpool audience found something to laugh at – Peter, inwardly shaking at the greatest 'near miss' of his life, had to get out of his skis, get back on stage and declare to the stunned cast – Paul Bown, Ivan Kaye, Stephanie Pack and Gillian Tompkins, "I'm a great skier, ja?" The audience roared their approval.

*Warwick Evans as the Sheriff of Nottingham, in Bill Kenwright's 1992 production of 'Robin, Prince of Sherwood'. Another example of a musical which Bill Kenwright used as a national tour for several years before returning it to the Playhouse, the second time as a Christmas production in December 1995. [Phil Cutts]*

**Fire.** Fire being the greatest fear in any theatre, several stories exist about incidents at the Playhouse which in reality were quite dangerous. On the very first night, 11 November 1911, while all the invited guests, the actors and staff were celebrating a successful opening night, with a late supper at the Adelphi, a fire broke out in the Manager's Office, front of house and very nearly pre-empted the dream. It had been started by a departing theatregoer throwing a cigarette butt into a bucket which had some debris in it. Fortunately the damage was confined to one room. Basil Dean, still at the theatre, had helped the Fire Brigade to put it out and consequently by the time he got to the Adelphi to reply to the speeches, his suit was streaked with dirt. One Guest of Honour, Miss Annie Horniman, just laughed, "Never mind, my boy, this is just the beginning".

Not all Fire Officers have given helpful advice to the various Stage Directors. During Eric Linklater's *The Atom Doctor*, Hugh Paddick had to make a round of toast, using a two-bar electric fire on the table. Charles Blair argued valiantly for the artistic necessity of this and was reluctantly given permission by the Fire Officer: "All right, it can stay, provided you've got a glass of water on the table to throw on the fire if the toast bursts into flame". Everyone held their breath as they realised what the man had said.

A member of cast left a lit cigarette in his dressing table which caused a fire, during Nigel Balchin's play, *Leader of the House*. Maud, phoning for the Fire Brigade, ordered them not to sound their sirens, as she had customers to consider, and they were not in any danger in her opinion. She is recorded as getting three full fire engines up Houghton Street, the firemen up to the dressing room in question and the fire put out, without any member of the cast, or audience, realising it.

Sometimes the in-house Duty Fire Officer was seen as a nuisance by staff not wanting a fuss made of 'minor' incidents, such as the time a fire started on stage in Cratchit's office during the 1969 production of *The Christmas Carol*. John Toogood, the stage manager, rang Cathy Alger and asked her to keep the fire officer of the time, Harry Reilly, busy, while they saw to things quickly and quietly! Harry was, at the time, inspecting the use of the irons in the wardrobe. Such details were part of a fire officer's brief for the safety of the building and personnel. In cases of emergency, his authority supersedes all others in the evacuation of the building.

**Problem Sets.** The use of silver, mirrors and other shiny objects can in fact be a disaster for the audience. It's one thing to have a flashing sword catching the light, but quite another if a static mirror is not dulled or someone produces silver lamé cushions which blind the audience. The story is told, from the Kay Gardner production of *Vanity Fair*, how at the last minute, after the final dress rehearsal, she asked for silver cushions for a boudoir scene which had a set dressed entirely in silver and black. May Finch and her assistant worked hard and all was in place as the curtain rose on the evening performance. However, the audience was dazzled by these cushions, and they had to be removed at the interval. Several press comments embarrassed all concerned.

But glittering swords are accepted as a fact of life and there are many sword stories that periodically do the rounds in Repertory. Nowadays, with fewer costume dramas, the art of stage swordplay is becoming increasingly dangerous. On one occasion, during *Robin, Prince of Sherwood*, Warwick Evans had to avoid serious injury by falling off the high slopping structure, designed by Bill Kenwright, in order to avoid a protagonist who seemed to have forgotten the planned sequence of the fight. People gasped, thinking he was hurt, which he was, but he later said he preferred a bruise to an open wound. Earlier sword memories, detailed at the theatre, did not always end quite so happily.

John Franklyn-Robbins here recounts a terrifying story from the February 1969 production of *Macbeth*:

*"An incident which brought a tear to my eye … the last fight is based theatrically on such terrible bitterness that it can affect the cool heads of the actors. Not so in this case I think, but disaster struck nonetheless. In early rehearsal the fight with big broadswords went well – fast, exciting and safe. But at the dress rehearsal it suddenly lost its rhythm and we found it hard to maintain the tension and climaxes; and so into performance. One night, just before my death, I was, according to plan, on my knees; a mistake was made; the point of my opponent's sword lay a foot in front of my face. I waited for the next stroke – a cut to the head. But without warning he lunged. The rounded end of the heavy sword folded my left eyelid back and went on into the back of the eye-socket. My sight was saved by a wonderful eye surgeon called Tom Phillips. [By some miracle Tom Phillips' son was in fact playing the part of one of the children in the play and, young as he was, realising what had happened, notified the wardrobe mistress, Cathy Alger, who was able to see that Mr Phillips was contacted.] The story in the daily press made much of the legend of bad luck surrounding the play, … but the truth – my opponent could not see three feet without glasses! Anthony Tuckey, full of concern, took the book and played while I was away."*

Michael Poole, the MacDuff, remembers it as, "the most terrifying moment I have spent on a stage, not to mention what JFR must have felt". He describes the whole production as living up to the reputation of 'the Scottish Play'. Other disasters mentioned against this self-same production included, Anthony Tuckey, the Artistic Director, who, while standing in for John, managed to break his big toe, causing the wardrobe department to buy a larger pair of boots. He then appeared on stage with one size eight and one size ten boot. None of the audience seemed to notice. But then, neither did Barbara Ewing who had to retire from the show with congestion of the lung, nor Sally Lewis who had to take on Barbara's part, nor the actor who should remain nameless, who was late for his call when his watch stopped while he was playing the fruit machines in an arcade. All this reinforces the general superstition against mentioning the actual name of this play.

Les Lyons recalled how during the 1988 production of the Scottish Play a broad sword left its mark on the building, rather than someone's face. McDuff's blade flew from its scabbard and nicked the Dress Circle, before burying itself in the seat of G7 in the stalls. Thankfully it was a dress rehearsal and the seat was vacant, but the nick may still be seem in Stanley Adshead's plaster work on the front of the Dress Circle.

Even rehearsals for sword fights are fraught with emotion and aggro. It can be very tiring, concentration is necessary, one slip could be lethal. But Bernard Cribbins remembers an occasion when they were rehearsing for *Cymbeline* in 1953:

*"… some students were in, being Roman Soldiers and Ancient Britons. There was a large battle scene and the things we were given to use were almost certainly like authentic Roman short swords weighing about two pounds each, brass handles, steel blades and people were just hacking about, one guy had his cheek laid open, another guy got a cut across the hand, and it all became rather dangerous and nobody seemed to be co-ordinating it at all. So William Lucas and myself got hold of everybody and taught a very basic 'clunk-clunk-clunk' type of swordplay which worked quite well, even if not very spectacular to look at, at least it was safe. One of the guys I was fighting had a rush of blood one evening and was hacking away and I really was sort of defending myself. At one point I managed to trap his sword above our heads and hold him and I gave him a swift knee in the crutch and ran off stage. I folded him up completely and the next night he went back to being very careful …"*

*Robert James as 'The Atom Doctor' by Eric Linklater, 1952, directed by Willard Stoker. [loaned by the family of Susan Withers]*

**Guns.** Andrew Sachs is remembered for the gun that would not go off. During the John Galsworthy play *Loyalties*, the villain of the piece locks himself in a bedroom and commits suicide by shooting himself. In fact Andrew, working as an ASM, was in charge of the blank-loaded firearm. In one unforgettable performance, the gun failed to go off. Andrew could hear the police inspector repeatedly saying, "It's no use, sir, you'll have to come out!" Eventually hearing the Inspector whisper, "Drop it, Andy, I'll cover it," followed by a dramatically declaimed, "Don't go in there – it's not a pretty sight! Blood everywhere!" Andrew felt the gun go off inadvertently in his hand. It brought the house down.

**Fire iron incidents.** One of the most repeated memories of older people in Liverpool is the sudden draught and the smell of greasepaint which seemed to almost overpower them, as the iron went up.

On more than one occasion, the fire iron (safety curtain) has given trouble during a performance. By law, it must be lowered at least once during an interval, to check that it is still working correctly. The Playhouse front iron is believed to be certainly as old as one hundred years, if not older. The company which maintains it believe it to be the oldest on their books. Originally water-powered and hand-operated, its hydraulics are now controlled from the prompt side of the stage by the simplicity of electric power.

One remembered mishap with the old water-powered system was during the 1947 *King Lear*, when during a matinee the iron started to slowly come down of its own volition. Nobody could do anything about it and it took twenty minutes for it to reach the ground. The performance had to be stopped. The pelmet which covers the lower part of the fire iron, when it is raised, limits the vertical lines available to designers. A set which caused a problem was that for Alan Beasdale's, *Down the Dock Road* [1976]. John Challis remembers that happier memories, such as working with the newcomer, Mickie Finn, and the joy of visiting Anfield, are somewhat overshadowed by the memory of having to bend almost double as the set design left half the audience unable to see the upper part of his body. Whoever designed it did not reckon with John's height, or the depth of the pelmet.

**Other mechanical problems.** Paul Williamson mentions a revolve which stuck, despite the best efforts of the large, strong stage-hand in charge. Indeed so many revolve stories exist that they cease to be funny to ASM's and Production Managers alike, but the audience at Liverpool has always been tolerant of mechanical malfunctions, except for the *Medea* collapsing wall which frightened many people. During the 1995 *Medea* tour, which featured Diana Rigg and Tim Woodward, the back wall of the set was supposed to collapse as a noisy representation of the tragedy and grief unfolding within the story. For nearly a week the crew struggled to control a complicated and dangerous structure, watching anxiously as the local boys, playing Medea's sons, were left standing perilously close to danger. Then, at least twice, most of the audience sat bemused while Diana Rigg continued her lines, hidden by the structure's refusal to collapse on cue, which left a solitary Tim Woodward staring up at the ghostly voice of Diana Rigg coming from behind the wall. For the boys, Ryan Jones, Michael Harriss, Adam Booth, and Mark Arends, it was a very frightening week but, as already mentioned, a chaperone was always on hand to attend to them. When a dangerous set was in use she would stay in the wings, in case she was needed. When confident that her charges were safe, the chaperone would watch them on the TV monitor in the Green Room.

Lynne Yarwood is remembered as a young student designer who, like all such students, had written into their contracts that they

Christopher Bullock began as production manager and became the second longest serving theatre manager at the Playhouse.

**Opposite** The Mathew Street wardrobe was one of the largest stores in the North of England. It specialised in twentieth century historical apparel, in particular military uniforms and accessories. The photograph shows the room dedicated to the storage of costume shoes from the last century. Sadly the entire store was disbanded after the liquidation of the Company. [Garner]

may design a set, usually carefully selected by the producer to take account of the student's abilities. Lynne was appointed to design for *The Gingerbread Man* and set about things with a determined dedication. At the first production meeting, with all the technical stage gathered round her, Lynne explained her design and what it should achieve, finishing with, "And the house collapses!" For a few moments they all looked at her in silence until one brave soul asked, "And how does it collapse, Lynne?" She looked innocently at them all and said trustingly, "It collapses by magic, doesn't it?" Thanks to their inventive hard work and dedication, they gave Lynne her magic!

In 1967, during the preparations for the production of *Emma*, John Page painted a baby grand piano a rose pink colour. The piano was on loan from Rushworths Music Store and staff were not too impressed when later the piano was returned 'washed'. There was a prolonged silence as everyone in the shop looked from the crew to the scrubbed piano and back again, until a shop assistant said, "Oh, well, Mr Rushworth is the Chairman of the Playhouse Board, so it must be OK!"

A very young and very new Assistant Stage Manager once caused a great deal of consternation. The usual caramelised sugar water used to fill bottles for 'stage' drinking, are emptied immediately after each performance, to prevent the glass discolouring. No one can recall the actual production, but in the 1960s, a local firm had given real bottles of booze for the play's drinks cabinet display, with the offer of their finally being drunk during the last night party. Imagine everyone's horror at the sight of a very junior ASM pouring the real whisky and gin down the kitchen sink! It is recorded that only one and a half bottles were rescued.

**Get in and get out.** Putting a set together begins with a design idea, often no more than a drawing. Once the design is approved by the Artistic Director, the Production Manager then costs it for the Administrator. After all approvals for expenditure are received from the Board, the Production Manager organises purchasing details, workshop rotas and the final 'get in' or 'fit up,' and 'get out' or 'striking the set' details. In other words, putting the set up and taking the set down. He remains on call throughout the set building and painting time allocated. The rep had its own in-house Production Manager.

One story, from the 1962 period, is given of Christopher Bullock, who began his twenty year commitment to the Company as Production Manager. For the first 'fit up' of his jurisdiction, he sat astride a chair, centre front and watched the men at work. It took them three days. When they had finished, Chris gathered them together and they awaited his praise. Instead he said, "Next time you will do it my way and in one and a half days!" After that, he always had the respect of the men of the crew.

Christopher Bullock is honoured as the man who proposed the layout of the new development. He oversaw the building of the new paint frame and workshop, which made Liverpool Playhouse the only Rep Theatre in England with an on site workshop with a raked trolley access onto the main stage, via a side iron.

Apart from the Royal Opera House, the authors could not find another producing theatre with the facility to build a set alongside a stage and wheel it through as a complete set. Happily, in the new developments, this facility is being retained.

**Lighting and electricity is known by the code LX in all theatres.** There were 26 circuits on the stage carrying 2,500 watts each and 5 circuits carrying 5,000 watts each [this format and rigging is due for change in the 1999 restructuring of the stage]. All lanterns are serviced between shows. Before each performance, all lanterns are tested. There are 26 bars hanging from the rig, which are

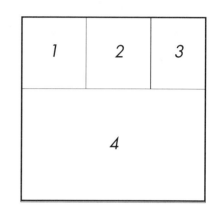

[1] Anne Marie Allison, wardrobe mistress 1980s – 1990s. [2] Cathy Alger, wardrobe mistress 1960s – 1970s. [3] May Finch, who began as wardrobe assistant under Susan Withers, seen here with Thomas Baptiste. [4] John Page, the in-house designer at a wardrobe fitting for 'Comedy of Errors'.

*Billy Meall's design for 'Billy Liar' by Willis Hall, 1996, directed by Richard Williams. [Loaned by Billy Meall]*

**Opposite** *The Billy Meall set for 'Billy Liar' with a youthful Paul Basson in the title role.*

used to carry the lanterns, scenery and hard or soft borders, which are used to mask the lights. Free-standing spotlights in the wings are masked by 'legs'. The curtains at the front of the stage are known as 'house tabs'. Whenever the house tabs or the fire iron are lowered or raised, outside a performance, safety is preserved by the call 'Tabs in' for down and 'Tabs out' for the raising up.

A memory of Jimmy Simmonds as a total technophobe and coping with people running backstage and shouting, "The Board's gone down!" was included on the Andrew Schofield tape. The pre-computerised board had many dimmer switches; it was positioned below the stage and demanded a careful co-operation between the LX and Stage Manager. Since the arrival of the microchip, the system is set up, lighting move by lighting move, during the technical rehearsal. It would be possible to set the programme running and leave it to work itself, except for the timing variations caused by audience applause, or actors corpsing. As the electricians, Gary Sanderson and Rob Beamer, tongue in cheek, once told a school party, "Pity we can't set the actors to speak at the same speed every performance and stop the audience clapping, then we could forget about the deck". That it is never as simple as that, has always meant that at least three electricians are needed most days, within the theatre. One begins the day checking all the safety aspects of the entire building; stage, backstage and front of house. The others spend time preparing the lanterns for the following production, rewiring, maintaining equipment such as the irons or electric saws, or drawing up plans for the lighting of a show, whether main stage or Studio.

Since the computerised system was introduced, the LX team have sat in the old bar area at the rear of the dress circle, where they have a magnificent view of the stage, both ahead of them and on a TV monitor.

The use of complicated sets is not an absolute must. A Shakespeare production is often at its best when performed upon a minimalist stage. Costumes are another matter altogether. Few plays are intended for naked presentation and when designed as such can cause considerable outcry. Equus is a prime example of this, as recorded in the Sue Wilson account of the 1974 production, when the criticism began even before the play was produced, and some mysterious poltergeist played havoc with the 'horses' velvet costumes … a mystery which still haunts the theatre to this day.

With an essentially middle-aged audience as the core component of Box Office statistics, nakedness will always be a contentious issue. If Alan Bleasdale got away with full frontal nudity in *Having a Ball* it was probably due to careful pre-sales marketing and posters which clearly stated the facts. *In An Awfully Big Adventure*, Tim Woodward was forced to be more circumspect in the incestuous sex scene. In rehearsal, neither the directors nor the cast had noticed just how 'naked' things could become. Other problems are outside everyone's control, such as when a naked man streaked up onto the stage during the John Chapman, Dave Simpson play, *I'm Marrying Robbie Fowler*. It was a full house and raised quite an amused laugh, when the audience realised that it was not part of the action of the play.

Not quite totally full frontal, but nevertheless an embarrassing experience, occurred during the 1979 production of *The Royal Hunt of the Sun*. Quite apart from the fact that February is usually one of the coldest months of the year and the actors, dressed only in black wigs and posing pouches, with full body make-up to cover the goose pimples, were already in the mood to demand danger money in case of pneumonia, it was also the silly season on bomb scares. Without warning, Derek Killeen, the Company Manager walked on stage and asked the audience to leave by the nearest exit. Turning to the actors he directed them, naked and shoeless, out into the cold night air, to gather with the public in Williamson Square. Michael Poole, David Beckett and Roger Phillips recalled this

incident. David gave the additional humorous comment that: "We provoked more than a modicum of native humour until finally we all repaired to The Queen's, a pub of outstanding hospitality. Failing to have any money in our posing pouches, it was, I'm sure, the first and last time Incas and Conquistadors have shared a pint with Scousers!"

Preparations for this production had previously provoked an anguished phone call from Liz Horrigan, Wardrobe Mistress, to one of her predecessors: "What measurements do we need for jock straps?" To be answered by: "Well, the first measurement you think of, you don't need!"

Beads are another commodity viewed with some trepidation. Not only do they make a garment heavy, they have a life of their own if they become detached or, as in the case of Marjorie Yates's memory of her professional debut, they detached themselves uninvited.

*"I was playing the local Madame Noseyparker and had to make my entrance through a beaded curtain. As I entered, my little handbag got caught in the beads and, pull as I might, I couldn't get free. The leading man, Peter Clay, finally came to my rescue and snapped the curtain – whereby the beads scattered all over the stage making a sound like a machine gun. A disaster which was duly reported in the 'Liverpool Post' the next day. Something about me making an 'explosive entrance' onto the Professional Stage!"*

In *Diary of a Scoundrel*, [1968] Penelope Keith suffered the embarrassment of wearing a felt dress, bright orange and with green trim, which she referred to as her 'carrot' dress. Jennifer Piercey, on the other hand couldn't get through the door in her dress, not even sideways. She is reported as being the first to say, "I've three dwarfs and a dog under here!"

Colin Baker, on the other hand, is fondly remembered for being the 'enfant terrible', both with the wardrobe department and the Company. Dressing up or undressing, Colin loved it all and his version of one of his famous tricks is recorded here.

*"While I was performing 'Christie in Love' in the Studio (1972), the main house production was 'The National Health' and the Christie cast were asked to be visitors in the 'ward' during the interval … we had carte blanche to make the visit what we could dramatically. On the first night I borrowed a friend's Old English Sheepdog and, with the help of a complicitous wardrobe department, I dressed as a pregnant woman and came on and harangued a supposedly dormant John Webb with shrill accusations of his being father of my vast unborn child … asked that my future appearances could be less vocal and extreme … my next persona was as an undertaker of the traditional and cadaverous mould. I was silent and inexorable. I measured each patient for their wooden overcoats and the keen-eyed might have been surprised to see poor John Webb develop a bad attack of the shakes whilst unconscious."*

Nowadays most theatre wardrobe departments prefer to use fur fabric, instead of real skins. Quite apart from the political issues now surrounding the use of real fur, the problem of insuring its use is astronomical. Probably the most expensive wardrobe item ever used on the Playhouse stage was a genuine mink coat loaned to the Company by George Henry Lee's, for a production of *Not Now Darling* in the spring of 1972. Jacqueline Morgan remembers the fuss surrounding the care of this coat. She says it had virtually a twenty four hour guard and she looks back upon its use with a sense of relief that Animal Rights Groups, then in their infancy, did not storm the stage.

Anne-Marie Allison was the Costume Designer and Wardrobe Mistress, 1979 – 1997: her shows, *The Pied Piper of Hamelin*,

**MRS SUSAN WITHERS**
An Appreciation

WARDROBE Mistress — Susan Withers." How many times has that phrase appeared on Liverpool Playhouse programmes? It is on the programme of the present production, "The Other Dear Charmer", and it will seem strange to have her name omitted when the next show goes up.

A fortnight ago, Sue—as we affectionately called her—eager to get on with the costumes for the play, arrived at the theatre early in the morning, and after going out to do a little shopping, came back, and collapsed at the stage door. She was rushed to the Royal Infirmary where, after making satisfactory progress for some days, she died suddenly yesterday morning.

We at the Playhouse will mourn her loss for a long time. There was no one quite like Sue. She was part of the theatre, where she came nearly thirty years ago to look for a temporary job, her husband being out of work owing to the slump.

She had had no training in theatre work but nothing daunted Sue. She was willing to learn, if need be by trial and error. After doing duty in the cloakroom, I asked her if she would like to be a dresser. Sue apparently knew what that in her kitchen at home—a useful piece of furniture! But when the duties were explained to her she willingly took on the job, and later was made wardrobe mistress, combining the two positions. Sue dressed all the women who have been in the

resident company from time to time, and many of them now stars—among them Diana Wynyard, Catherine Lacey, Rachel Kempson, Judy Campbell, Jane Baxter, Dorothy Reynolds never failed to pop into the wardrobe when visiting Liverpool. Marjorie Fielding and Muriel Aked, now both dead.

One of her most prized possessions was a gold wristlet watch presented to her by the Playhouse directors after twenty-five years' service. She was wearing it when she was taken ill.

By Sue's death I have lost a dear, faithful friend, and the directors of the theatre a loyal and servant, who gave herself untiringly to the Playhouse and was very jealous of its traditions.

MAUD CARPENTER.

*Wardrobe Mistress Susan Withers press cutting.*

**Opposite** *New lighting deck, showing the view of the stage during 'Only the Lonely' as seen by the 'LX' technicians. [Denis Garner]*

*Stanley Williams in his call-boy uniform of 1936.*

**Opposite** *Examples of winning entries in the 1954 programme design competition.*

*The Maroon Cortina, Not Quite Jerusalem, A Taste of Honey, Bedroom Farce, Nuts* and *Be Bop a Lula*, to mention but a few. However, her favourite of all was her work for *Beauty and the Beast* in 1985.

Some of the many small anecdotes, which added colour to the life of both wardrobe mistresses and actors alike, included the borrowing of £400 worth of real jewels from H Samuel, the jewellers, because the costume jewellery made out of wine gums would have looked awful in the press photographs. It was all returned the next day and the wine gums replaced with a strong adhesive.

Then John Toogood had to live down the embarrassment of announcing over the Tannoy, during the 1969 production of *The Comedy of Errors*, "Would all the nuns, in whatever state of dress or undress, please come on stage immediately."

**Stage Managers and ASMs.** The very first Stage Manager was Arthur K Phillips (1911 – 1916). He also acted, directed and wrote plays. Nearly all Stage Managers and ASMs have appeared on stage occasionally, even if only in Christmas plays or revues.

**Technical trainees.** At Liverpool Playhouse, from the very first days of the theatre, many aspiring actors came to work in any capacity. But, perhaps more importantly, it should not be forgotten that considerable numbers of quite young technical trainees and work experience teenagers, came from local schools and colleges to learn on site. In the later years, the organising of this voluntary, and often time-consuming task, was generously undertaken by Frankie Stokes, the PA to the Artistic Director. The demand for places often meant that applications had to be sent in anything up to a year in advance.

**Stage door.** Little is known or recorded about the original Stage Door Keepers. Public memory recalls being able to open a large green door and leave your programme on the shelf, for the actors to sign. There was definitely a less security-conscious attitude to backstage, partly because there was not the need for it and partly because the internal structure of the theatre meant that you could not proceed more than a few yards. There is some 'folk' memory of twin brothers who watched over the door and minor repair jobs within the theatre, but Stanley Williams names them as Michael and Tom Eagle and he did not believe they were twins. They certainly covered the 1930s period and helped with maintenance on a day to day basis. Sam Keeley, the 1980s maintenance man is probably the most typical of the breed who walked about with a small tool box and kept the theatre functioning efficiently. However, since the 1970s the office of Stage Door Keeper was transposed to that of a Receptionist's role. All phone lines and mail passed through their hands, admittance to the building was controlled by entry phone and the clocking in of domestic staff and others became part of their duties.

**Ushers and usherettes.** The longest-serving usherette – indeed the longest-serving member of staff ever – is recorded as Doris Houlton, who worked at the theatre for 58 years, 1925 – 1983 (beating Maud Carpenter's record by 7 years). Awarded the British Empire Medal, she retired at the age of 73. She is remembered for taking charge of the counter in the stalls Coffee Bar and the control of the centre aisle of the stalls. Pam Brooks recalls Doris recounting her bemused response to the actors' lack of ballroom dancing skills: "They can do the Twist, but they've no idea how to do a Waltz." Consequently, she gave them dancing lessons for the production of *Present Laughter*.

Many older people recall how they ordered their tea as they entered the theatre and the usherettes would come round with tea

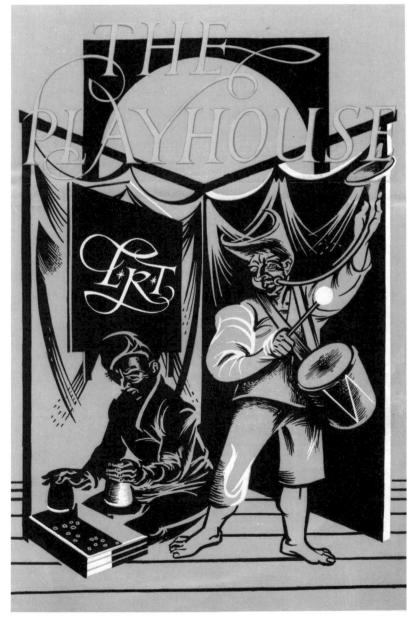

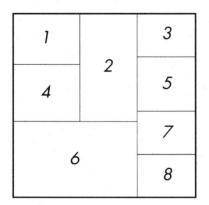

People at work in the theatre. [1] Car used in the 1963 production of 'Dr Knock'. [2] Helen Lindsay in a dress designed by Alan Pikford for 'Othello', 1955. [3] 'Affairs of State'. Early recycling of parts for sets and furniture! 1959. [4] Set design for 'An Elegance of Rebels' by Richard Marks, 1962. [5] Set design with tromp l'oeil for 'The School for Scandal', 1961. [6] Set design for 'The High Road' by Augustus Trout, 1932. [7] View of the set for 'Jouneyman Jack', designed by Candida Boyes and directed by Ian Kellgren. [8] The 'Wind in the Willows' car 1996 was on loan from Birmingham Repertory Company. [Phil Cutts]

trays, which you could clip onto the back of the seat in front. This practice was stopped probably in the late 1940s, early 1950s, an exact date is not recorded.

Carol Walker began her 21 year service as an usher, moving up through the ranks to Head Usher, to Front of House Supervisor and ending as Duty Manager, the 1990s title for Front of House Manager. Before her, a long list of affectionately remembered figures who were mostly recalled with some reference to a particular trait. Jenny Dunn always smiling, Yvette Bowen, the tall one!

**Crowd control.** Amongst problems faced by the ushers, early programmes show that ladies' hats continued for many years to be a major issue. Fashionable hats were too big, so we get a request in programmes for ladies to remove their hats, "... if respectfully requested to do so." Exactly what they were expected to do if the request was not respectful, was not specified.

As late as 1921, the problem of ladies' hats continues, this time with the request: "Will ladies please refrain from sticking hatpins into the backs of seats, as this causes damage and is expensive. As an experiment, patent hooks for hats have been attached to the back of a few Pit and Pit Stalls seats; if they prove popular, more will be added, with the hope that they will be of some convenience to our patrons and mean the cessation of sticking hatpins into the backs of seats."

The assumption that only men smoked in public allows for the accusatory 1920s programme request, "Gentlemen are requested not to fling their cigarettes on the carpets but to deposit them in the receptacles provided for that purpose."

In the 1930s in several programmes, in capital letters, is the following request: "PLEASE DO NOT STRIKE MATCHES TO READ YOUR PROGRAMME DURING THE SHORT SCENE CHANGES: IT IS A VERY DANGEROUS HABIT." The security of the theatre's patrons meant that, in modern times, ushers had to rehearse fire safety procedures on a regular basis, to ensure compliance with the City Council regulations. First aid and the care of children and patrons with disabilities were essential parts of the ushers' training days.

The sale of programmes has always been a duty for the ushers at The Playhouse. For the Christmas production of *The Sleeping Prince*, [21 December 1954] a programme cover was used which had won second prize in a countrywide competition sponsored by the Liverpool Playhouse. The winner was Mr Keith Hensby, aged 22, of Spalding, Lincolnshire. He had studied at the Lincoln School of Art.

Behind the scenes, often seemingly divorced from the public, there were managers, bookkeepers, accounts managers, press and publicity officials, programme and poster organisers, marketing and sales workers, outreach workers, secretaries, maintenance workers, security personnel, cleaners, the list is endless. However the name of a head cleaner from the 1960s and 1970s, Delia Keeley, pops up every now and again, as crew or cast mention how clean the place was kept in the old days, thanks to her. Perhaps people were less careless with their litter, but as Michael Williams [LX] recalls, Delia had once hit him on the bottom for standing on a chair with his shoes on and she had an air of 'authority' which meant you obeyed her. Her pride in having a sparkling theatre was very evident to all who knew her.

It is perhaps important to mention, with gratitude, the countless businesses, such as Zane and Christine Billal of Gateacre Press, Phil Cutts the photographer, Kevin Tiernan and many, many more who, in their time became, vital to the life of the Theatre and who were sadly and severely financially affected by the final liquidation of the Company. Their loss of income can never be compensated. Many who were associated professionally or just as theatre lovers with the Playhouse, continue to feel a sadness at the number of small companies affected. The final chapter of this volume tries to explain some of the issues that preceded closure.

# Proposed Liverpool Repertory Theatre.

A meeting at which Professor C. H. Reilly, Professor Ramsay Muir, Messrs. Ronald Jeans, Alec Rea, Cliffo. Muspratt, George Rathbone, J. J. Shute, Basil Dean and F. R. Martin were present took place at 4 p.m. on t. 5th April 1911 at Liberty Buildings Liverpool.

It was proposed and seconded that Professor Reill. take the Chair and it was carried unanimously.

After a lengthy discussion relating to the propose. purchase of the Star Theatre and the proposed bui. of a Theatre on a site in Colquitt Street and the acquisition of the site at the corner of Brownlow S. and Mount Pleasant for the purpose of the erec. of a new Theatre It was decided to adjourn. meeting until Wednesday afternoon next at 4 o'c. ... and request

## Chapter Nine
## THE ACHILLES HEEL

Successful financial control within a theatre company must begin with a budget that allows for reasonable expenditure on the commodity, the production of plays. The most successful time in the Rep's history was under the Chairmanship of Lord Cohen (1949 – 1960). Eight of those years had six-figure profits, six of them exceeding Richard Williams' 1997 record of £110,000 (£114.400 in 1998 values).

Lord Cohen was an avid reader of play scripts. He helped to develop the selection process and actively vetoed work he believed to be inappropriate. His secretary, Miss Terry [Lily] Lanceley, as well as James Rushworth, referred to Lord Cohen's extensive knowledge of work by living writers. He was instrumental in bringing, amongst others, Arthur Miller's work to the Playhouse.

**Costing production.** It can take as few as three unprofitable shows close together, in any one season, for the house of cards to be threatened with total collapse. This principle seems simplistic, and possibly is, but throughout the entire history of the Playhouse it has been proven as a sequence to warn of an impending crisis. Any building-based theatre company would agree that such a run casts an ominous shadow.

> Typical costs of Repertory production during the 1990s
> **Studio** between £15,000 and £30,000
> **One-set productions on the main stage** between £40,000 and £60,000
> **Two-set productions on the main stage** between £70,000 and £110,000
> **Musicals with one set on the main stage** between £90,000 and £130,000
> **Musicals with more than one set on the main stage** add £30,000 per set
> **Building maintenance,** approximately £1,000 per day for heating, lighting, insurance, security, repairs and maintenance

**Value for money.** The 1997 RSC touring production of *Cyrano de Bergerac* had a subsidy of over £300,000 and still lost money, in spite of increased ticket pricing and selling to full capacity at all venues. Bill Kenwright's production of *Ferry Cross the Mersey* was budgeted for production at £143,184. Because of its popularity, a five week run and slightly higher ticket pricing, it was accorded a financial success in the local press. Yet in terms of what was needed to maintain the theatre, it could still, because of its high production costs, not be regarded as 100% profitable. Provincial repertory theatre companies know that they cannot compete with the likes of the national theatres in London and Stratford.

**Outside influence.** The table of Companies House records, at the end of this chapter, illustrates that there was never a static end-of-year result. Variations to these figures are frequently, and with some justification, blamed upon outside influence such as the national economy, social upheaval, time of war, political forces such as bomb scares or bus strikes, or alternate interests such as the World Cup.

**Stability 'In-house'.** A more careful examination of the accounts also allows for the argument that internal Company activity could, on occasion, be equally contributory to the various crises that have hit the Company. The stability brought about by Colonel Shute, once he was joined by Maud Carpenter and William Armstrong, would set a precedent for success – namely that where at least two of the top three management, ie. Chairman, Administrator and Artistic Director, were compatible in terms of management principles, then

---

The best end of year profits, as converted to the Bank of England's equivalent contemporary values of the pound.

1. 1951 £163,850
   *Cohen – Stoker – Carpenter*

2. 1950 £160,000
   *Cohen – Stoker – Carpenter*

3. 1948 £159,369
   *Shute – Fernald – Carpenter*

4. 1952 £152,970
   *Cohen – Stoker – Carpenter*

5. 1954 £120,496
   *Cohen – Stoker – Carpenter*

6. 1956 £118,936
   *Cohen – Stoker – Carpenter*

7. 1997 £114,400
   *Landau – Williams – Dawson.*

8. 1955 £110,730
   *Cohen – Stoker – Carpenter*

9. 1953 £103,091
   *Cohen – Stoker – Carpenter*

10. 1922 £98,213
    *Shute – Armstrong – Carpenter*

11. 1957 £63,437
    *Cohen – Stoker – Carpenter*

12. 1958 £59,911
    *Cohen – Stoker – Carpenter*

*Opposite 1911 minutes – a page from the first meeting of the Company.*

reasonable control of spending could be maintained. Similarly, it is not difficult to establish the conclusion that the best years usually followed a minimum of 40 weeks, in-house production with a full resident company.

**Public subsidy.** A retrospective study of the Company displays evidence that once public subsidy came upon the scene, its continuance became the major administrative nightmare facing the Board, and a deceptive security blanket used by many producers to push for more production finance, whether in cast sizes or bigger sets. It also, with some justification, allows the public to argue against increases in ticket pricing.

**Shifts in power structures.** Constant pressure from funding bodies had considerable influence upon in-house policies, most notably in the extending of Outreach and Youth Theatre services. These were often used as benchmarks for success by local authorities, as the emphasis for approval of subsidy shifted away from mainstage work. From the theatre's point of view, Outreach and Youth Theatre work was frequently a placatory gesture towards the five local authorities, who never fully subsidised it and eventually it added to the Board's headaches.

There was gradually an eroding of the Board's autonomy. Board members ceased to be recognised figures both within the building and within the city. James Rushworth and Henry Cotton were the last of the chairpersons to have any real political power and that at considerable cost to themselves, as they fought with outside funding bodies and the problems from the residual debts of the 1966 building programme.

However, the 1986 abolition of Merseyside County Council can, in retrospect, be seen as the single most contentious issue in the story-line behind the external events that led to the closure of Liverpool Repertory Company. Research has not shown any venues in other regions facing such a problem. It appears to be peculiar to Mersesyside, affecting also the two other major recipients of Merseyside public subsidy, Liverpool Everyman Theatre and the Royal Liverpool Philharmonic Society. All found themselves in the unenviable position of dealing with five local authorities: Liverpool, Wirral, Sefton, Knowsley and St Helens. The annual contribution offered by each borough was not always consistent. Neither was it necessarily approved by the Arts Council in its demand for parity of contributions from local authorities. In Merseyside, the straightjacket of public subsidy has had a complexity all of its own.

At the Playhouse, debts arising from problems of funding have always been designated within the Company as 'historic debts'. This differentiates them from 'production debts' or 'Inland Revenue debts' and what was later known as the 'debt of honour' which became due to Bill Kenwright Limited.

From the 1970s and 1980s, there were discussions on the question of competition from the Everyman. Many have since come to believe it was non existent, or if it had been remotely true, would have been better ignored. There was never any real competition. Each theatre caters for its own predominantly loyal clientele, and so it has remained to this day. Nothing could more clearly illustrate this truth than the fact that when the Playhouse was closed, for whatever reason, 90% of the Playhouse audience base has always headed out to Mold, Chester or Manchester. The Playhouse's prolonged closure of 1998 – 1999 has not made any appreciable difference to the returns at the Everyman. For the future it will be interesting to watch the proposed amalgamation of the two theatres into one company to be called The Liverpool and Merseyside Theatre Trust.

Fairness requires that attention should be drawn to other issues that affect all theatres in the seesaw of financial burden, most particularly the growth of the large scale musical genre, especially the London-produced multi-million pound versions, which are increasingly being toured to large Provincial Theatres. As such projects are seldom one-off self-financing productions, theatres need to reassess the economic sense of trying to emulate the style of these huge ventures, in theatres with a limited box office capacity, or a restrictive funding policy.

Carl Hawkins, as Chairperson at the time of the 1983 *Blood Brothers*, had some justification in sanctioning such an expensive production. History has given its own verdict on the value of that decision. History can also say of such ventures, that they have changed public taste just as much as, and maybe even more than, the influence of the more frequently blamed TV and film industry.

Within months of *Blood Brothers*, Carl Hawkins and Bill Morrison had begun their plea for help by stating in the *Liverpool Daily Post* on the 24 July 1984, that the Playhouse history is a living history. To quote from the article by Philip Key entitled, *Curtain looms over theatre*:

"*Liverpool's Playhouse Theatre will close its doors in January unless it gets more money. The warning was given last night by the Playhouse chairman, Carl Hawkins. The theatre, which made an £89,000 loss in the last financial year, is seriously underfunded. Artistic Director, Bill Morrison, said the debate always would be whether people wanted to see the historic theatre continue as a place where artists could work. 'Don't confuse our efforts with the true issue, the living history of a Playhouse in which we are temporary sparks of light … I believe we could attract even more (audience) if we could bring our prices down to the level which, in the present climate of Merseyside, would allow people to come regularly instead of occasionally. Of course, this kind of policy, of making theatre available to all, at the price they can afford, is at the heart of the idea of public subsidy – and without sufficient subsidy we cannot pursue it.*"

Bill Morrison referred to his position as 'a temporary spark of light' and it is a beautiful idea, since hundreds of individually talented sparks would light up the stage and burn brightly forever. But perhaps the voices of history would have said, better to cut your cloth to fit, rather than continually beg because you are chasing an artistic dream.

As discussed in Chapter Four, Ian Kellgren certainly chose to follow an adventurous, some would say ambitious or visionary approach which, while it respected the more traditional audience of the Repertory, meant that he nevertheless felt compelled to challenge not only his own artistic skill, but that of others. He was prepared to allow Kate Willard to develop the Youth Theatre to its historically highest point of achievement. Most notably, he gave his support to Willard's founding of the now internationally respected Brouhaha Festival. Then there was an aura about some of the work of the talented directors used, particularly the associates, Kate Rowland and Peter Oyston. Some productions, such as Peter Oyston's *Madame Mao*, in November 1989, were expensive and regrettably provided insufficient return at the box office, at a time when Kellgren's own well-praised *Great Expectations* in December 1989, was in need of cross production funding support. This accumulating of production debt from the 'roll-over principle' is hard to accurately pinpoint from the perspective of hindsight. But, when a season's programme is planned, it is always dependant upon a multiplicity of expensive and unknown factors: costs such as publicity, programme and poster printing, royalty fees, music fees, designers, the weather, bomb scares, the death of a president or just inner city access problems caused by long term road works! The list is endless. To cancel is sometimes a dearer option! To proceed always a risk! Only large scale producers weather the unpredictable storms that are frequently consequent upon long term commitment to a stated programme. Six months is the maximum a theatre the size of the Playhouse is usually able to plan for and hopefully complete.

Following *Great Expectations*, the Company was well into the next season's preparations and once again they came to that impasse synonymous with cash flow problems linked to Funding battles. There is a certain irony of fate, that had William Fulton and the Board not been in the throes of dealing with yet another funding issue, they may well have weathered that particular storm. Through the computerisation of the box office system, they were now monitoring, not only audience reaction, as mentioned previously, but also the available daily purse. Surviving a further twelve months, thanks to a bank loan, they did not pick up the flak until during the autumn 1990 season, when another delay in funding finally took effect. They tried, they took the risk. The promised level of funding did not materialise and when the box office fell yet again, they knew enough of the history of the Company not to take any further risk.

Ian Brown, an Arts Council Drama Officer, writing in 1991 in *The Stage* Newspaper, puts the other side of the story, when he says that, "The Arts Council is tired of being told it should bale out stricken clients willy-nilly". He draws attention to the need to find a policy that is "constantly aware of strategic and creative need" and not one that only responds to every immediate crisis.

Whatever the truth of the Arts Council's commitment to the Playhouse during this period, the Board had no choice but to opt, in January 1991, for Administration. They were merely ahead of the game. Every theatre was in the same mess, thanks to national arts policy changes over which theatre companies had no control.

Barry Dale was the 1991 appointee Chairperson. He was, more often than not, unable to attend meetings and eventually handed the Chair over to Malcolm Landau. Much of the unwieldiness caused by the presence of experts was removed in the lean, and supposedly mean, newly-formed Board. William Fulton rightly remained; his contribution to the acquiring of business sponsorship had always been successful. Elizabeth Christie and Ian Kellgren also remained, Christie's legal expertise being of invaluable service over many years of the Theatre's history. Bill Kenwright, the London impresario, was set up as Executive Producer with Ian Kellgren as the in-house Artistic Director.

In 1991, Bill Kenwright was seen as a reasonable option by the Official Administrator, Frank Taylor, and all other funding authorities. The management team at Bill Kenwright Limited and the various departmental representatives at the Playhouse, were not always clear as to the extent of the commitment undertaken. At first things seemed to be working. How much of this was based upon contractual detail and how much upon the good will usually synonymous with 'a gentleman's agreement', will never be fully ascertained. As the months progressed, neither the Board nor Bill himself were without some justifiable complaint.

Prior to the period of Official Administration, Ian Kellgren already had a working relationship with Bill Kenwright which had proved fortunate during the campaign to save the Company. Kenwright was able to bring in three plays already touring under his Company label. As these works had been produced elsewhere, the cost to the Playhouse was greatly reduced. Momentarily beneficial to all concerned, but deceptive in that the non-theatre authorities, such as local authority officials, thought most, if not all Kenwright productions, would be along similar financial targets.

Bill, meanwhile, vigorously undertook the task of bringing a more West End style to the theatre from April 1991 – April 1996. Although not present on site, his was, like Leslie Lawton before him, a dominant and charismatic presence to the public mind's eye.

'Too Good To Lose', – 1991 campaigners outside the Arts Council of Great Britain. Younger members of the Save the Playhouse team of 1991, left to right: Dougie, Gill, Geoff, Beverley, Corinne, Rodney and Gary. They were received by Mr Charles Hart to whom they presented more than 20,000 of the total of 126,000 signed postcards petitioning Lord Palumbo, the Arts Minister. [Friends of the Liverpool Playhouse Archive]

He said the use of his *little black pocket book* was his greatest contribution to Liverpool theatre as it gave him access to so many famous names. Unfortunately, after his statement in the 1991 brochure, when he wrote, "... my role as Executive Producer gives me virtual control of the theatre's fortunes ...", he had publicly placed himself in the unfortunate position of being assumed responsible for just about everything which took place at Liverpool. And few remembered at this point the warnings from 1921 – 1922 which Grace Wyndham Goldie amply summed up as:

> "The choice lay between the life and death of the theatre. The choice of life means that there are many great plays which some of the directors, the producer and a section of the theatre's supporters would like to see staged which will have to be put on one side: that the producer has often to spend his great abilities in putting on small things well, instead of noble things finely: that the company has often to act slickly when it is capable of acting greatly. Yet for a theatre to be a vital part of the life of a great city is in itself a great thing; and in touching the lives, in affecting the taste, of numbers of people, the theatre may be achieving finer things than if it gave the greatest plays for the enjoyment of a clique."

At first very popular with the audience, Kenwright's programming later had its critics. He suffered from some disasters such as *Sienna Red* or *The Cabinet of Dr Caligari*. Equally he had some apparently successful box office returns with his many musical biographies. But, balanced against expenditure, the wonder is that such expensive productions continued to be presented.

The blurring of accounts between the Playhouse and Kenwright's office, the question of the level of shares from tour royalties and the overspending on certain productions, became daily issues between the Bill Kenwright Company and the Playhouse. The first real battle was over the 1992 *Blood Brothers* production which came out over three times the original production costs estimated. This, and many similar examples of increased expenditure, were seldom ratified by the Board. On the one hand, the unrealistic perception of Bill as, 'the man who is going to save the Playhouse, come what may' and on the other, as, 'the man who did just as he pleased', does justice to neither side in the situation. Bill himself was seldom the negotiator in brokering the situations which arose; he and the Board have had to cope with the embarrassment caused in their names.

Then there was the even more contentious issue of where Playhouse staff loyalties lay. Kellgren was frequently the 'piggy in the middle' of the situation and his health was obviously suffering. He was advised to take a sabbatical, following which, he returned to direct the December 1994 *A Christmas Carol* as his final engagement with the Company.

With no in-house Artistic Director, there was a growing atmosphere of distrust that left Bill Kenwright even more in the role of an 'absentee landlord'. Delays in communication were bound to occur. This did little to help either side. Eventually he had to admit a weariness with the disputes over money. He is quoted as saying, "If I can't do it, I doubt if anybody can!" Retrospectively, not being resident in-house must surely have been one of his most significant weaknesses – or difficulties, depending upon the camp in which your loyalties lay. Bill Kenwright, in the *Look Alive* magazine of August 1986, had prophetically declared himself as not being equipped for running a theatre building. To quote from page 16, "I'm not a buildings man, I'm a people man. The best way I could help theatre in Liverpool was to be on the outside and let people who know how to run theatre – run it." On that occasion he rejected the offer to buy the Empire!

By 1996, the demand for maintenance of such an elderly building was putting increased pressure upon the Playhouse Board. They were seeing little return from the Box Office for basic domestic expenses. The Board was also under pressure from the Arts

Council to make a decision which was in fact, – choose between being a commercially-run theatre or a subsidised theatre. Choose between Kenwright or subsidy!

Bill Kenwright was informed his contractual commitment to the theatre was not to be renewed. That he had felt the pressure, no one can doubt. Companies House records show that he did not receive his intended annual management fee on a regular basis and this was to accumulate, to become known as part of the final 'debt of honour' which the Board labelled as his due. Others believed his accounting system more than compensated Bill via the 'in kind' aspect of his use of the workshops, wardrobe, sound and lighting equipment. Certainly there is no evidence, in the Companies House records, as to the claimed level of his underwriting of the Box Office. However, history will, and should, remember Bill as a man who tried when the chips were down! The sad truth is that by April, 1996, the Playhouse was left with nearly a million pounds of debt, one half classified under either 'historic' or 'production' debts, a further quarter owed to Kenwright himself as the 'debt of honour' and the rest, nearly a quarter of a million pounds, directly attributable to the non payment of Inland Revenue during 1995 period. The exact sequence of events around this debt may not be discussed in any real depth here, but it is evident that the relationship with the Inland Revenue was, during that period and for whatever reason, a very fraught tightrope for all concerned. The first indication of the Inland Revenue's intention to wind up the Company was presented to the then Theatre Director on the 14 September 1995 and in the November a final demand for payment in full was received from them. Various delays and prolonged discussions finally resulted in a proposed re-payment schedule in July 1996 and for a short while the situation appeared stabilised.

The Bill Kenwright Limited departure also meant a change of personnel within various departments of the Repertory Company. The first to be appointed in 1996 was Richard Williams, as the Artistic Director. A Liverpudlian who, having begun his own theatrical career at the Playhouse, was aware of its true history. He returned to the very roots of Repertory and successfully made it work, just as William Armstrong had done in 1922 following the departure of Nigel Playfair. Once again there was to be 'one last chance.' Williams' modus operandi, of mixing the entertainment factor with the educational and paying more attention to the local needs of the community, meant that the audience slowly began to trust him. Richard Williams, in the course of eighteen months, re-introduced a resident main house company, returned to a lower expenditure level, and used in-house designers, creative workshop and wardrobe whenever possible. For the first time in ten years a hope for survival seemed a reality. The debts, under the management of Anne Morris, were being reduced and this period helped bring about the seventh most successful end-of-year profit in the Company's history – a great achievement in the face of overwhelming odds, including much unwarranted criticism. Richard Williams deserves to be praised, for he was a courageous person, and a talented director, who deserved a better chance than he was given at Liverpool.

**The coup de grâce.** So, who fired the arrow at the Achilles Heel? Where does the buck stop? Whatever the mismanagement of the relationship between the Arts Council, the Board and Bill Kenwright Limited, there will always remain some unanswerable questions. The truth may never be known. Each side believes it has right on its side. Each side made mistakes of judgement. The Arts Council never admits to a mistake! The Board has had to admit theirs!

The debt to the Inland Revenue from the 1995 period was being paid off in instalments under various agreements, as was the 'debt of honour' to Bill Kenwright. However in January 1997, faced with insufficient funds to cover both of these debts, the Board

'Without the customer, what is theatre?'
The one-millionth customer: Henry Cotton presents Mrs E Jones with a bottle of bubbly 18 March 1981.

made the fateful decision to allow an Inland Revenue instalment to lapse. This meant that the whole Inland Revenue debt immediately became due in its entirety. There was to be no more negotiation. No more re-negotiation! Full settlement of the debt to the Inland Revenue was demanded, making the final closure of the Company inevitable, since no help was forthcoming.

Triumph and tragedy are the hallmarks of drama. The story line leading up to the final denouement is more significant than the sword thrust of the coup de grace. Admittedly, the primary ironical aspect of the plot line is its most recurring headache, public subsidy! First seen in 1963 and still hanging like a grotesque albatross around the management's neck in 1997. However, if time-consuming subsidy battles were a basic underlying ingredient of the disaster, it must also be said that a growing reliance upon subsidy appears to have become another significant figure in the equation. From 1991, the Board appears to have failed to seriously energise itself towards other money making schemes. Successful external business sponsorship became less evident. Whether this was being withdrawn because Kenwright was perceived, rightly or wrongly, as an 'In-house man with money' and therefore the commercial interest contolling the theatre, or whether it was due to sponsors' own lack of financial resources generally, is unclear. But one thing is clear, that from 1991, until the appointment of Richard Williams in 1996, the achieving of greater savings, through control of production costs, is not evident. Without a doubt, this does appear to be due to the complexity of the arrangements, for the artistic management of the theatre, as imposed by the Official Administrator, the Arts Council and all others concerned with the 1991 process of Administration. Had the policy of true Repertory been re-imposed, at that time, it is doubtful that the Company would have closed in 1998. As Grace Wyndham Goldie had stated in 1935, the size of the building itself was, 'at once a cause of the theatre's success and a limitation set upon its activity'. It was never designed to be able to emulate the West End, nor to finance the dreams of ambitious men. It belongs to the people, the ordinary people of Liverpool and Merseyside.

Only now are people recalling these sensible words from Maud Carpenter, here quoted, from an unassigned press cutting in the archive, "A simple philosophy … in the ever-changing world of theatre … strict budgeting: loyal audiences: drawing up the year's programme to include the adventurous and some money makers. And being content to make a living and not a fortune". Applied to a company it makes sense and, if followed through, self reliance should be possible.

As a listed building, the theatre remains, it still has the breath of its history whispering through its corridors, in its dressing rooms, on its stage, and most importantly, in the excitement of every child visiting a theatre for the first time. It is, and always will be, 'An Awfully Big Adventure,' no matter from which side of the foot-lights you sense its great past.

We wish it well, even as we mourn the loss of the Liverpool Repertory Company whose spirit echoed through the Playhouse making the building itself world renowned. We mourn the loss of that system which created such a great theatrical tool for the education of actors and local community alike. We are all of us the poorer for its passing.

# ANNUAL PROFIT AND LOSS
## As given at Companies House, Cardiff

Accounting policies have varied with time, but the figures quoted here are the amounts stated in the annual Directors' Reports as the profit or loss on the year, taking into account all income, grants or subsidies and after all charges. Mortgages or accumulated debts are not reflected in these figures. The right hand column shows the equivalent contemporary value in July 1998.

| Year | Chair | Administration | Director | Profit | Loss | Profit/loss at 1998 value |
|------|-------|----------------|----------|--------|------|---------------------------|
| 1911 Mortgage set at £10.000 | | | | | | |
| | Reilly | Jallard/Amour | Dean | | | [£467,100] |
| 1912 | T Piggott | | | | [-£231] | [-£10,626] |
| 1913 | J Shute | Edwards | Hanray | | [-£385] | [-£17,710] |
| 1914 | | | McIntosh | | [-£1,402] | [-£64,392] |
| 1915 | | T Piggott | | +£91 | | +£3,367 |
| 1916 | | Danson | Pratt/Adams | +£686 | | +£21,266 |
| 1917 | | Jerome | Bellamy +2 | | [-£1440] | [-£37,440] |
| 1918 | | S Piggott | | +£831 | | +£17,451 |
| 1919 | | | Leslie/Wilcox | +£3,251 | | +£68,271 |
| The return to peacetime increased audience figures | | | | | | |
| 1920 | | | Wilcox | | [-£100] | [-£1,800] |
| 1921 | | | Playf/Drewitt | +£331 | | +£6,620 |
| 1922 | | Carpenter | Armstrong | +£1,133 | | +£28,325 |

This 1922 figure was only achieved on paper by drawing upon the reserve account to cover a true loss of [£1,363]. The theatre was set to close, when the team of Shute – Armstrong – Carpenter took control in 1922. From this point until 1962 the method of accounting is relatively consistent. A reserve account was re-opened, which eventually provided for the maintenance of the building and the losses of World War 2 and ended with providing the financial base for the extension of 1966.

| Year | | | | Profit | | Profit/loss at 1998 value |
|------|--|--|--|--------|--|---------------------------|
| 1923 | | | | +£609 | | +£15,834 |
| 1924 | | | | +£208 | | +£5,408 |
| 1925 | | | | +£443 | | +11,581 |
| 1926 | | | | +£403 | | +10,478 |
| 1927 | | | | +£381 | | +£10,210 |
| 1928 | | | | +£905 | | +£24,661 |
| 1929 | | | | +£648 | | +£18,144 |
| 1930 | | | | +£447 | | +£12,963 |
| 1931 | | | | +£537 | | +£16,566 |
| 1932 | | | | +£198 | | +£6,225 |
| 1933 | | | | +£62 | | +£2,027 |
| 1934 | | | | +£277 | | +£8,708 |

| Year | Chair | Administration | Director | Profit | Loss | Profit/loss at 1998 value |
|------|-------|----------------|----------|--------|------|---------------------------|
| 1935 | | | | +£384 | | +£12,072 |
| 1936 Mortgage cleared | | | | +£682 | | +£21,039 |
| 1937 | | | | +£600 | | +£17,520 |
| 1938 | | | | +£696 | | +£20,323 |
| 1939 Roof repaired | | | | | [-£686] | [-£19,674] |
| 1940 Outbreak of WW2 | | | | | [-£944] | [-£23,382] |
| 1941 Closed by war | | | | | [-£3,556] | [-£80,756] |
| 1942 | | | Various | | [-£1,691] | [-£38,402] |
| 1943 | | | | +£265 | | +£6,018 |
| 1944 | | | | +£1,600 | | +£36,800 |
| 1945 | | | | +£1,740 | | +£38,976 |
| 1946 | | | Fernald | +£2,008 | | +£44,356 |
| 1947 | | | | +£675 | | +£4,910 |
| 1948 | | | | +£7,699 | | +£159,369 |
| 1949 Major roof repairs done | | | | | | |
| | Cohen | | Cross | +£570 | | +£11,508 |
| 1950 | | | | +£8,222 | | +£160,000 |
| 1951 | | | Stoker | +£9,118 | | +£163,850 |
| 1952 | | | | +£9,356 | | +£152,970 |
| 1953 | | | | +£6,496 | | +£103,091 |
| 1954 | | | | +£7,739 | | +£120,496 |
| 1955 | | | | +£7,382 | | +£110,730 |
| 1956 | | | | +£8,364 | | +£118,936 |
| 1957 | | | | +£4,617 | | +£63,437 |
| 1958 | | | | +£4,471 | | +£59,911 |
| 1959 | | | | +£3,444 | | +£44,772 |
| 1960 | | | | +£4,697 | | +£61,061 |
| 1961 | Trustam | | | +£2,742 | | +£35,646 |
| 1962 | Rushworth | Hamilton Moore | Hepton | +£305 | | +£3,660 |
| 1963 Arts Council grants began | | | | | | |
| | | | Scase | | [-6,870] | [-83,510] |
| 1964 | | | | | [-£849] | [-£10,188] |
| 1965 | Cotton | Gardner | | | [-£3,131] | [-£34,597] |

| Year | Chair | Administration | Director | Profit | Loss | Profit/loss at 1998 value |
|------|-------|----------------|----------|--------|------|---------------------------|
| 1966 | | | | +£3,227 | | +£34,270 |
| 1967 | | | Gardner | | [-£2,420] | [-£24,200] |
| 1967 Bus strikes severely affect box office | | | | | | |
| 1968 | | | | | [-£521] | [-£5,163] |
| 1969 | | Bullock | Tuckey | | [-£262] | [-£2,462] |
| 1970 | | | | | [-£1,753] | [-£15,777] |
| 1971 | | | | | [-£9,013] | [-£72,465] |
| 1972 A break even end of year | | | | | | |
| 1973 | | | | | [-£5,991] | [-£41,937] |
| 1974 A break even end of year | | | | | | |
| 1975 | | | Lawton | +£2,998 | | +£14,990 |
| 1976 | | | | | [-£1,753] | [-£7,345] |
| 1977 | | | | | [-£2,998] | [-£10,822] |
| 1978 | | | | | [-£42,778] | [-£139,884] |
| 1979 | | | Gaunt | | [-£16,518] | [-£47,571] |
| 1980 | | | | | [-£19,496] | [-£47,765] |
| 1981 | | | Bond +3 | | [-£14,496] | [-£31,746] |
| 1982 | Hawkins | Beddoes | | | [-£27,280] | [-£54,832] |
| 1983 | | | | | [-£44,250] | [-£85,402] |
| 1984 | | Fischel | | | [-£89,498] | [-£163,781] |
| 1985 | | | | +£39,798 | | +£68,850 |
| 1986 | | | Kellgren | | [-£16,932] | +£28,276 |
| 12 May 1986 records detail a conversion of a Merseyside County Council loan to a grant in the 1985 period | | | | | | |
| 1987 | | | | | [-£106,587] | [-£170,539] |
| 1988 | Fulton | | | | [-£78,747] | [-£120,482] |
| Board set in motion a sponsorship campaign and 1989 figures show how effective it was for the Rep | | | | | | |
| 1989 | | | Stalker | +£,688 | | +£,976 |
| 1990 | | | | | [-£322,391] | [-£419,108] |
| 1991 | Dale | | Kenwright (Kellgren) | | [-£224,629] | [-£274,047] |
| 1992 | | Redmayne [temporarily] | | | +£52,350 (Nine months only) | +£61,773 |

Companies House records show that the Board waived a debt of £152,920 (£180,445) owed by Kenwright to the Rep

| Year | Chair | Administration | Director | Profit | Loss | Profit/loss at 1998 value |
|------|-------|----------------|----------|--------|------|---------------------------|
| 1993 | | | | | [-£178,810] | [-£207,419] |

| Year | Chair | Administration | Director | Profit | Loss | Profit/loss at 1998 value |
|------|-------|----------------|----------|--------|------|---------------------------|
| 1994 | Landau | | | | [-£183,034] | [-£206,828] |

Kenwright was paid £74,255 on his management fee: the only year he was paid, but he then had to spend £100,00 (£113000) to underwrite a weak Box Office

| Year | Chair | Administration | Director | Profit | Loss | Profit/loss at 1998 value |
|------|-------|----------------|----------|--------|------|---------------------------|
| 1995 | | Dyszkant | | | [-£73,913] | [-£81,304] |

After five years Kenwright was owed £271,624 (£298,786), and the non payment of Inland Revenue returns increased tenfold and added over £200,000 to the accumulated debts of the Rep.

| Year | Chair | Administration | Director | Profit | Loss | Profit/loss at 1998 value |
|------|-------|----------------|----------|--------|------|---------------------------|
| 1996 | | Parry [temporarily] | Williams | | [-£310,285] | [-£332,004] |

£35,000 from Kenwright to underwrite a Box Office debt. Richard Williams took over in the April, inheriting an approximately £1,000,000 debt. The Board negotiates to repay 'Debt of Honour' to Kenwright, ie. the unpaid management fee originally asked for in 1991 when he came to 'save' the Playhouse.

| Year | Chair | Administration | Director | Profit | Loss | Profit/loss at 1998 value |
|------|-------|----------------|----------|--------|------|---------------------------|
| 1997 | | Dawson (April) | | +£110,000 | | +£114,400 |

Jane Dawson's appointment as Administrative Director only took effect from April 1997, two months after the fateful Board decision had been taken concerning the Inland Revenue debt. During the last nine months of the Company's life, she backed Williams' return to repertory principles in Liverpool with significant success. The year ended with a profit, but insufficient to settle the Inland Revenue debt.

3 January 1998, thus the closure of the Company came as it was completing its seventh most successful year in the 86 years of its history.

*The 1974 production of 'The Contractor' by David Hare, directed by Sue Wilson. The cast had to learn how to put up and take down a marquee on stage.*

# Behind the scenery

**Administrative**
Marion Armstrong
Jean Beed
Jo Brabner
Anne Bradshaw
Patricia Breen
Morag Brooks
Gill Cooper
Susanne Corrigan
Julia Donat
Anne Evans
Michael Gaunt
Victor Glynn
Pamela Gray
Janet Gunnery
Jacqui Home
Brian Howard
Steve Hughes
Marian Kong
Debi Jones
Kathryn MacDonald
Kate Massey
Alan McCracken
Joanna McKeever
Michaela Nicholson
Sharon O'Toole
Amanda Revers-Higgins
Carolyn Sims
John Stalker
Frankie Stokes
Walter Sudell
Karen Syme
Simon Tompsett
Sue Thompson

**Production**
Di Stalker
Robert Longthorne
Mary Loise Lauder
John Claus
Katherine Sandys
David Butterworth
Griselda Dick
John Whewell
John Toogood

**Company Managers**
**Stage managers and ASMs**
Simon Jessel
Tracey Alizon
Don Harley
Maris Sharp
Billie Klinger
Stephen Court
Brian Barton
Vicky Jackson
Yvonne Annis
Lennox Killner
Alison Love
Brian Regan
J Rice Cassidy
J Gordon Fleming
Howard Leslie
A Douglass
Leo Montgomery
Sidney T Pease
James Whale
Charles Bristow
Edwin Greenwood
Jane Bullock
Harold Bowerman
Stuart Dornford-May
Nick Waters
Helen Wilding
David Bartlett
Graham Hindle
Chlôe Furnival
Philip McCandish
Christopher Whatmore
Sally Woodland
Liz Burton
Debar Hardy
Maria Taylor
Cara Cavanagh
Vicky Jackson
Gell Dove
Pip Horobin
Helen Aquis-Kelley
Virginia Llewwlyn
Debra Hardy
Denise Walker
Emma Bingham
Sarah Percival
Fiona McCallion

Cath Lill
James Leatherby
Kate Roud
Katrina Gilroy
Mel Moran
Christine Chadwick
Barry Holmes
Nicholas Shearman
Annabel Ingram

**Carpenters / stage crew**
James H Baxter
Paul Barry
Alan Roberts
Michael Andrews
Paul Russell
Alan Howe
Richard Ashby
Jimmy Duffy
Martin Cody
Terry Marlowe
Paul Dring
Pat Grimley
Antony Peaker
Mark Scott
Richard Prior
George Smith
Richard Baxter
Gary Hesketh
Simon Veness
Dave Murray
Charles Brent
John Phillips
Jo Topping
Roger Rahn
Brian Hopkins
William Squirrell

**Electricians / LX**
Kevin Fitzsimmons
Robert Longthorne
Clem Rawling
Leslie Lyons
Jimmy Simmons
Richard Sharratt
Steve Lomax
Brian Kendrick
Ralph David

Carrie-Anne Stevens
Michael Williams
Gary Sanderson
Rob Beamer
Nick Toale
Ian O'Donoghue
Dave Guy
Joanna Town
Andrew Waddington
Alison Thorpe
Jo Weeks
Mark Rickards
Jayne Bell
Will Simonsz
Alan Michie

**Designers and scenic artists**

| | |
|---|---|
| George Harris | 1911 |
| Doris Zinkeisen | 1921 |
| Augustus Trout | 1920 – 1930s |
| Ronald Trout | 1930s |
| Paul Mayo | 1940s – 1950s |
| Betty Gow | 1950s |
| John Burnand | 1950s |
| Alan Pikford | 1950s |
| Donald McKinley | 1950s |
| Inigo Monk | 1959 |
| Richard Marks | 1960s |
| Martin Morley | 1970s |
| Jonathan Porter | 1970s |
| Claire Lyth | 1970s |
| Liz Horrigan | 1970s |
| Alison Waugh | 1970s |
| Richard Sumner | 1970s |
| Voytek | 1980s |
| Andy Greenfireld | 1990s |
| Phil Cutts | 1980s |
| Bim Hopewell | 1980s |
| Candida Boyes | 1980s |
| Andy Greenfield | 1980s |
| Billy Meall | 1960s – 1990s |
| Les Brotherston | 1990s |
| David Collis | 1990s |
| Chris Rehill | 1990s |
| Will Simmons | 1990s |
| Jocelyn Meall | 1990s |

## Costume Designers

| | |
|---|---|
| Burkinshaw's | to 1940s |
| Carl Bonn | 1950s |
| John Burnand | 1950s |
| Alan Pikford | 1950s |
| Inigo Monk | 1950s |
| Richard Marks | 1960s |
| Bim Hopewell | 1980s |
| Anne-Marie Allison | 1980s – 1990s |
| David Hollis | 1990s |

## Wardrobe

(Often not listed, in the early days)

| | |
|---|---|
| Mrs King | 1915 |
| Miss Burns | 1930s |
| Miss Don | 1930s |
| Susan Withers | 1940s – 1950s |
| Marion Agar | 1950s – 1960s |
| Jan Hughes | 1960s |
| May Finch | 1960s – 1970s |
| Cathy Alger | 1960s |
| Shelley Brian | 1970s |
| Alison Aacaule | 1970s |
| Anne McMurray | 1970s |
| Liz Horrigan | 1970s – 1980s |
| Charlotte Bird | 1980s |
| Joanna Sim | 1980s |
| Anne Marie Allison | 1980s – 1990s |
| Heather Brocklesby | 1990s |
| Denise Walker | 1990s |
| Andrea Forde | 1990s |
| Gillian Lyons | 1990s |

## Stage door receptionists

include
Stephanie Anderson
Eileen Leckie
Laura White
Susanna Turner Wilson
Christine Duffy
Caroline Lunt
Eloise Attwood
Anne Pope
Melanie Dodd
Paul Currie
Alan Mercer
Sally Hobson
Barbara Sandison

## Box Office

Maud Carpenter
Patricia Breen
Catrin Williams
Kelly Marie Smith
Alison Ball
Brendan Carroll
Ivan Wadeson
Lisa Bilby
Ian Perry
Kathryn Stevens
John Stevens
Dolly Cottier
Nuala Hamilton
Lyndsy Eccleston
Paul Myatt
Joan Burnett
Alison Oxlade
Victoria Stevenson
Samantha Suggate
Elaine Taylor
Eloise Attwood
Alice Bennett
Fiona McCallion
Ian Perry
Victoria Allen
Nuala Hamilton
Bekki McCormack
Sam Fear
Katie Jones
Nicola Stevens
Joan Neill
Betty Culbert
Barbara Moore
Audrey McPherson
Winifred Parry
Andrew Stokes

## Front of House

Doris Houlton
Desmond West
Matthew Calderwood
John Dennis Sloan
Jenny Dunn
Yvette Bowen
Yvonne Garriock
Gloria Ashworth
Debra Ashworth

Rebe Rathbone
Viv HUghes
Lisa Walker
Chris Trigg
Kate Stewart
Steve Threlfall
Ian Tayler
Ray Hazlehurst
Frank Mullen
Margaret Halpin

## Ushers and Front of House

Doris Houlton
Desmond West
Matthew Calderwood
John Dennis Sloan
Jenny Dunn
Yvette Bowen
Yvonne Garriock
Carol Walker
Gloria Ashworth
Mary Lauder
Kate Stewart
Steve Threlfall
Gill Collinson
Tom Gilmore
Ann Gilmore
Jean Mills
Vivian Hughes
Rebe Rathbone
Chris Trigg
Beryl Smith
Lisa Walker
Dawn Obodo
Geof Regan
Beverley Clark
John Stevens
Sue Pugh
Ian Taylor
Ray Hazlehurst
Frank Mullen
Kate Potts
Heidi Boyle
Kal Ross
Lee Wymer
Keiron Breen
Helen James
Anna Lieb

Eunice Tamblin
Margaret Rhodes
Margaret Halpin
Ben Turnbull
Marie Turnbull
Anne Robinson
Ivy Curtis
Noreen Clinton
Jan Armour
Margaret Williams
Barbara King
Joan Chidlow
Lisa Walker
Andrew Bradley
Joanne Black
Tracy Nichols
Claire Prenton
June West
Karen West
Yanna Groves
Sheila Blackburn
Eve Blackburn
Tracy White
Michelle Byatt
Paul Byatt
Elouise Attwood
Katy Jones
Ann Pope
Len Simcock
Brian Regan
Geraldine Lee
Jessica Lee
Nicola Ellis
Paula Forshaw
Marina Marshall
Dave Marshall
Susan Hayes
Alan Richards
Sarah Childs
Pat Roxburough

# INDEX

*Basil Dean at the Golden Jubilee celebrations, 1961.*